The Sporting News

presents

NOLAN RYAN

From Alvin to Cooperstown

SP
SPORTS
PUBLISHING
INC.

www.SportsPublishingInc.com

3 1984 00237 5887

Coordinating Editor: Rob Rains
Developmental Editors: Joanna L. Wright, Terrence C. Miltner
Director of Production: Susan M. McKinney
Interior Design: Scot Muncaster
Interior Layout: Michelle R. Dressen
Dustjacket and Photo insert design: Terry Hayden

ISBN: 1-57167-258-3

Printed in the United States

www.SportsPublishingInc.com

CONTENTS

CHAPTER 1

WARMING UP

NOLAN RYAN

Lynn Nolan Ryan, Jr., of Alvin, Texas, played his first full season of professional baseball in 1966 for the Greenville (South Carolina) Mets. He had spent the end of the 1965 season with the Mets' Appalachian League team, and reported to St. Petersburg over the winter for the Florida Instructional League. When he threw his first pitch, he acquired the fireballer reputation that would stay with him forever. In 1967, a former teammate of Ryan's made the following prediction about the young pitcher: "When he gets the curve over for a strike, he will be another Sandy Koufax."

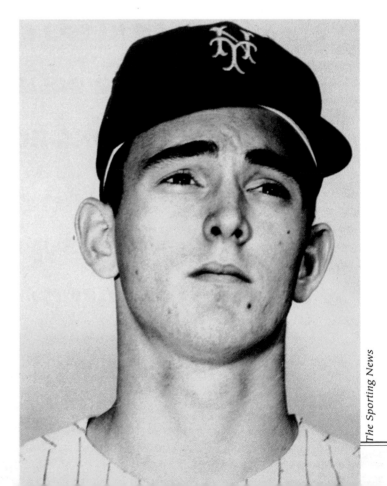

RYAN RACING TO FLASHY START AS MET GREENIE AT GREENVILLE

by JIM ANDERSON **MAY 28, 1966**

GREENVILLE, SOUTH CAROLINA—Two years ago, Lynn Nolan Ryan, Jr., was pitching for the Alvin High School team in Texas, was dating Ruth Holdorff and dropping by the Dairyland or Oasis for a snack after a movie.

That's the full excitement for teenagers in the town of about 10,000 people in the oil country—20 minutes' drive from Houston.

Now Nolan Ryan is in his first full season of organized ball, wears the uniform of the Greenville Mets and ranks as one of the parent New York club's top mound prospects.

He started the Western Carolinas League season by tossing 25 scoreless innings and, in six games, compiled 62 strikeouts and a 4-0 record.

Ryan began pitching eight years ago when an older brother, a catcher, needed someone to pitch to him at home.

"I guess he made me a pitcher," Nolan said of his brother Robert, now an Air Force lieutenant in Okinawa.

Nolan went through Little League ball to the Babe Ruth League and on to the high school team in Alvin, where his father is supervisor with the Pan American Petroleum Co. In high school, he pitched two no-hitters and his prep record was 20-4. "The only thing I had was a fastball," he said.

Murff Spotted Talent

Mets scout Red Murff first saw Ryan pitching in his junior year.

"He seemed to see something in me no one else did," said Ryan.

Ryan pitched Alvin to the runner-up spot in the Texas Triple A baseball playoffs. Needing to win the last two games from Waxahachie, Nolan pitched a two-hit, 2-0 shutout and tried to come back the next day and start again. He was lifted in the first inning because of wildness.

After the playoffs, he was drafted by the Mets as a free agent.

"I wasn't sure I was going to sign," he said.

"Several colleges had offered me scholarships and I was planning on going to Sam Houston." But Murff talked Ryan into signing for a modest amount.

"Now I'm glad I signed," said Nolan. "Now that I've been in baseball, I like it better than I thought I would."

Ryan reported late to Marion, Virginia, in the rookie Appalachian League last year. He appeared in 13 games and had an unimpressive 3-6 record and 4.38 earned-run average. But he struck out 115 batters in his 70 innings.

Nolan knew he had a control problem when he reported to the Florida Instructional League at St. Petersburg last winter. Working with him were coach Bunky Warren and Murff.

"They had me throw more overhanded," he said. "It helped my curve a lot. I believe I picked up speed. I know I got a lot more confidence." A change-up pitch was added to his assortment and increased his effectiveness.

Needed Fattening Up

Ryan weighed only 155 pounds when he signed. Eddie Stanky, then director of player personnel for the Mets, had him drink rich things along with eating all he could.

"It didn't help," he recalled.

He now carries 168 pounds on his 6-2 frame and can't add another pound no matter what he eats.

Greenville manager Pete Pavlick knew early at spring camp in Homestead, Florida, that he wanted Ryan for one of his pitchers. Pavlick had managed Ryan at Marion and was impressed by the youngster's winter showing at St. Pete.

Nolan will have to go into the Army Reserve six-month program next winter. Whatever time he has in the off-season will be spent bird-hunting with his pointer, "Harry Thomas."

Oh, yes, and dating Ruth Holdorff with stops at Dairyland or the Oasis in Alvin.

SONS OF ERIN—FITZ AND RYAN—PROMISE EMERALD MET FUTURE

by BARNEY KREMENKO **SEPTEMBER 24, 1966**

The closing week of the 1966 season finds Mets manager Wes Westrum testing the luck of the Irish, and if things work out as Wes hopes, he sees his club's future that much greener, with no pun intended.

Among the young players brought up at the end of the minor league season for an advance look are two sons of Erin getting particular attention—outfielder Shaun Fitzmaurice and right-handed pitcher Nolan Ryan.

Fitzmaurice is a 24-year-old Notre Dame graduate who batted a measly .219 for 61 games at Jacksonville of the International League at the outset of the season, but then wound up at .316 for 64 games in Williamsport of the Eastern League, a notch below I.L. competition.

"I was over-matched in Jacksonville, but I found myself in Williamsport and now I believe I am ready for any company," he said.

That's what Westrum wants to find out. As a fielder, Fitzmaurice comes with the highest recommendation. He also brings speed, having been a sprint star at Notre Dame.

Ryan, after a year and a half in organized baseball, has established himself as a strikeout king with an impressive set of figures. For 280 innings since turning pro, the tall, gangling 19-year-old from Alvin, Texas, shows 422 strikeouts.

At Greenville in the Class A Western Carolinas League this year, he had a 17-2 won-lost record, fanning 272 in 183 innings.

From there he went to Williamsport, where he was 0-2, but fanned 35 in those two games. One of his defeats was via a 2-1 score, a ten-inning affair in which he struck out 21.

Westrum didn't plan to start Ryan, but did want to give the kid a few chances in relief.

"Sure he's young and inexperienced," the Mets' manager pointed out. "But you never can tell. Every now and then a fellow comes along who's ready early."

Ryan went on the Mets' 40-man roster shortly after finishing up in Williamsport and joined the club for its final Coast trip. To make room for the slim Texan (he's 6-2 and 170), another young pitcher, Jerry Hinsley, was placed on the restricted list. Hinsley is awaiting a military draft call.

Other young players being looked at down the homestretch were shortstop Darrell Harrelson, catcher Greg Goossen and outfielders Danny Napoleon and Johnny Lewis.

Another recalled pitcher, Darrell Sutherland, was to get a starting chance.

"We've used him strictly in relief before," Westrum said. "It could be that he's better geared for starting."

The big concentration, though, was on Fitzmaurice and Ryan. They were completely new to Westrum and the Mets' skipper wanted to find out as much about them as quickly as he could.

INT. BATTERS BLINDED BY SMOKE —IT'S ROLLING OFF RYAN'S HUMMER

by BOB PRICE   **JULY 1, 1967**

JACKSONVILLE, FLORIDA—The noise Nolan Ryan is making around the International League is big—even for a Texan.

The 20-year-old native of Alvin, Texas, hasn't started a game for the Jacksonville Suns, but his fastball is the talk of the league.

Ryan is just out of the armed services and he had 17 strikeouts among the first 20 outs recorded while he was on the mound.

Ryan fanned eight Syracuse batters, getting the final seven in a row, on June 4. Three days later, in Rochester, Ryan struck out nine in four innings.

Striking out the opposition isn't anything out of the ordinary for the 6-2, 175-pounder.

Back in his high school days, he was feared by all foes.

After being signed in the Mets' organization by Red Murff, a former Jacksonville manager, Ryan struck out 115 in 70 innings of competition in the 1965 Florida Instructional League.

Ryan opened the 1966 season at Greenville, South Carolina, in the Western Carolinas League, but was soon promoted to Williamsport (Eastern). Before he left, he was 17-2 with a 2.51 earned-run average. He struck out 272 in 183 innings.

At Williamsport, he joined manager Bill Virdon, now the skipper of Jacksonville. Ryan set an Eastern League record for an extra-inning game by fanning 21 in ten innings. He got 19 in nine innings, matching a feat recorded earlier at Greenville.

> **"I had to catch him in the Rochester bullpen without lights. I chased as many as I caught. He can really throw smoke."**

Ryan's six-month service hitch ended in mid-May and he reported to the Mets' Winter Haven (Florida State) farm club.

There's one big difference between Ryan and most young fastballers. He isn't wild. And when he does miss his mark, it's usually with a curve.

Ryan, who is on the shy side, laughs off his fastball with a story of his high school days. He relates, "In a game one day, I hit the first batter on the head. I got the next one with a pitch on the shoulder.

"Then the third batter went to his coach and told him he didn't want to bat."

When you say Ryan is the big talk of the International, you can quote such figures as Dale Long, the former major league home-run hitter and now an umpire in the I.L., Rochester manager Earl Weaver and Virdon.

"You don't see any better at his age," said Long.

"When he gets the curve over for a strike, he will be another Sandy Koufax," said former teammate Jackie Warner.

"It's hard to tell how fast Ryan is right now. Wait until he has made three or four starts. Then maybe you can tell," said Weaver.

Warner explained his respect for Ryan's speed this way: "I had to catch him in the Rochester bullpen without lights. I chased as many as I caught. He can really throw smoke."

RYAN WHIFF SAGA A FABLE? METS WONDER

by JACK LANG   **MARCH 30, 1968**

ST. PETERSBURG, FLORIDA—Rube Walker was seated in the left corner of the dug out, which he figures was the best vantage point for his first look at the Mets' No. 1 phenom. Beside him sat two reporters and then Gil Hodges, who was flanked on the other side by a minor league rookie named Mike Figueroa, who never opened his mouth.

It was the unveiling of Nolan Ryan, the Mets' fabled minor league strikeout whiz. People were beginning to think Ryan was something of a myth. They've been hearing about him for years, but few have ever seen him pitch except in places like Marion, Virginia, Winter Haven, Florida, and Greenville, South Carolina. In those towns, he's an immortal.

In Jacksonville, Florida, they still think Ryan is a myth. Nolan had pitched three times in relief for Jacksonville last summer, striking out 18 batters in seven innings. All games were on the road. Then they announced he would pitch at home. More than 6,000 turned out to see the "new Bob Feller." In Jacksonville, 6,000 fans is like 60,000 in Shea.

"I felt a pain in my elbow warming up and when I told Bill Virdon, our manager, he advised me not to pitch," Ryan related.

"When they announced I was unable to pitch, I was in the clubhouse but they tell me the fans really booed."

Kept Under Wraps

Ryan never pitched again last season after feeling the twinge. He was with the Mets all September when they were looking at every prospect in the chain, 27 of them in all. But they wouldn't look at

Ryan. Wes Westrum was under orders not to pitch him.

Hodges got his first and only look at Ryan in one game in the Florida Instructional League in October. And it was a very brief look. He knew he'd see a lot more of him in the spring.

But when the Mets' batterymen arrived here February 20, Ryan wasn't among them. He was doing a military hitch and didn't show up until a week later.

When the squad games were played, Ryan didn't pitch. "He reported late and he's behind everyone else," Hodges explained.

Reporters with the Mets as well as the columnists who travel around the state were beginning to believe Ryan was a myth.

The announcement that Ryan would start a "B" squad game against the Dodgers brought out a half-dozen nationally syndicated sports columnists, another dozen ordinary reporters, four or five cameramen, plus a couple hundred senior citizens.

The big moment finally came and sure enough there was a Nolan Ryan. He was out on the mound, ready to face some kid named Bill Grabarkewitz.

Ryan wound up and here it came...his first pitch.

It was a high fastball and as it zoomed in, the batter swung after the ball was past him.

Rube Walker turned to the two reporters on the bench and whistled softly in admiration.

"Boys, let me tell you something. That pitch had a little 'hurry' on it," he drawled.

It seemed every pitch Ryan threw had a little "hurry" on it. Grabarkewitz, with two strikes on him, finally managed to pop to short center, where Don Bosch came in and made a fine catch.

But Luis Alcaraz looked at a third strike and Willie Crawford swung at a third strike.

Swingers Look Bad

Between innings, Walker told Greg Goossen, who was catching, to call for more curves and change ups.

Len Gabrielson flied to left with two strikes on him to open the second and Ryan threw a curve and caught Tom Hutton looking at strike three for the second out. He ended the inning by making Jimmy Campanis look bad swinging at strike three.

In two innings, Ryan had faced six men and struck out four of them. He was no myth.

Nolan came over near Walker for a drink of water while the Mets were at bat. Rube asked him how the arm felt and the kid said it was a little tight up in the muscle area. But trainer Gus Mauch said it was nothing to worry about since it was in the front and not the back.

So Ryan, who said he was all right, went out to pitch the third inning. He walked Ken Worthington on four pitches, but Larry Eckenrode popped to second on a hit-and-run and Washington was doubled off first.

Tsuneo Horiuchi, the little Japanese pitcher who was hurling for the Dodgers, had two strikes on him when he finally popped to Art Shamsky for the third out.

Arm Trouble Returns

Ryan had pitched three hitless innings, faced nine men and struck out four of them.

Hodges was quite pleased and impressed.

"He not only was fast, but his curve was exceptionally good," the manager said.

Walker was still shaking his head after it was over.

"Boys," he raved, "that man is outstanding!"

A few days later, Hodges wanted to give Ryan his second test. Nolan was named to pitch the middle three innings of a game against the Pirates.

Ryan pitched one mediocre inning, giving up a run on two walks, a hit and a sacrifice fly. But he never came out for the second inning.

"His arm tightened up in the forearm," Hodges reported. "Maybe he has to pitch some more to strengthen it. I don't know. We'll have to wait and see."

Once again, Ryan was put back under wraps with a puzzling arm injury. In less than a week, he had felt pain in his biceps muscle and pain in his right forearm.

Even Johnny Murphy, the general manager of the Mets, began to wonder if Ryan wasn't some sort of a myth.

It was the unveiling of Nolan Ryan, the Mets' fabled minor league strikeout whiz. People were beginning to think Ryan was something of a myth. They've been hearing about him for years, but few have ever seen him pitch except in places like Marion, Virginia, Winter Haven, Florida, and Greenville, South Carolina. In those towns, he's an immortal.

NOLAN RYAN

CHAPTER 2

IN THE BIG APPLE

Seeing was believing for the Mets' pitching coaches. They finally got an up-close look at their minor league strikeout phenom. From the amazing depths of a struggling expansion franchise in 1968 to the Miracle Mets of 1969, Ryan saw it all. But he saw a lot of it from the bench and the bullpen. Everyone who watched him pitch knew he had the talent to become a great pitcher, as he set and reset the Mets' strikeout records. However, military commitments and injuries kept him from a regular job in the starting rotation for the Mets, and he was traded in 1971 to the Angels.

Minor league strikeout king Nolan Ryan works out under the watchful gaze of Mets pitching coaches (left to right) Wes Stock, Rube Walker Eddie Yost and Yogi Berra.

Daily News

HODGES RATES RYAN WITH KOUFAX, BARNEY AS FIREBALLER

by JACK LANG   **APRIL 13, 1968**

Take it from Gil Hodges, this kid Nolan Ryan is in a class with Sandy Koufax, Rex Barney, Sam McDowell, and Karl Spooner. Gil mentioned all four of those names after he got his first good look at Ryan and he was referring to the sheer velocity of Ryan's fastball.

Will he ever be as good as Koufax...cause as much frustration as Barney and McDowell...or fade into oblivion the way Spooner did? Hodges wouldn't venture a guess.

"All I can tell you is that the boy has a great arm," Hodges said.

"I had heard about it, but I had never seen it. Now that I have, I believe it."

This was after Ryan had pitched against the world champion Cardinals, in a produce-or-else game.

> "All I can tell you is that the boy has a great arm. I had heard about it, but I had never seen it. Now that I have, I believe it."

"I can't keep waiting for him until he's ready," Hodges had said. "If he's going to make this team, he's going to have to show me what he can do. He isn't going to make the team on his reputation."

Ryan's reputation is for his strikeouts in the minor leagues. In 291 innings with assorted Met farms the kid from Texas had whiffed 291 batters. But he also frequently came up with a sore arm after pitching.

Muscular Pain

This spring, Ryan reported late because of another Army call, and was immediately behind all the other pitchers and not ready until mid-March. When he finally did pitch, it was in a "B" game. His three innings were impressive, but a pain developed in the bicep muscles. When he finally pitched again, it was only one inning in a varsity game. This time the pain appeared to be in the forearm.

Finally, on March 26, it was put up or get lost. Ryan started against the Cards at Al Lang Field and there are some people who won't forget it.

In four innings, Ryan struck out six batters... including Orlando Cepeda, Johnny Edwards and Mike Shannon in succession in the second inning. As he strode off the mound after that startling performance, the 1,916 senior citizens on hand rose to give him a standing ovation.

He also made an impression on the Cardinals.

After the game, Cepeda tabbed Ryan as "the best young pitcher I have seen since I came into the major leagues."

Lou Brock was equally impressed.

Lou Went Defensive

"He blew me away from the plate," said the league's No. 1 base thief. "He made me strictly a defensive hitter the second time up."

As he went to the outfield after striking out in the first, Brock joked with coach Eddie Yost.

"Why doesn't that kid work on his change-up?" Brock asked.

"What surprised me," said Hodges, "was his control. Do you realize he pitched only 11 innings last year and he didn't walk anyone in this game?"

A few days later, Hodges planned to pitch Ryan in a game against the Braves. Again he was unable to look at him. But this time it wasn't any pain in the arm. This time it was a weekend Army stint that forced Ryan to miss his regular turn.

In an attempt to prevent blisters when throwing, Ryan resorted to soaking his fingers in pickle brine, a remedy suggested by Mets trainer Gus Mauch (right).

PICKLE JUICE SWEETENS LIFE FOR RYAN

by JACK LANG

MAY 18, 1968

Whether or not he wins any other honors in his freshman year, Nolan Ryan is almost certain to be named "Man of the Year" by the Pickle Packers of America. In two weeks, he has done more for the pickle industry than Peter Piper, the guy who picked a peck of pickled peppers, ever dreamed of doing.

Ryan has made pickle brine famous as the new elixir for pitchers with blistering fingers. There's a supermarket in the Bronx that proudly advertises, "Mets' Pitching Juice Sold Here." And all because Nolan Ryan dips his tender ol' finger in the pickle brine.

Word had been out only a few days that Ryan was using pickle brine when a rival pickle company called the Mets and offered to donate five gallons of the juice. Trainer Gus Mauch, who made the ten-cent investment that started the whole thing, declined with thanks.

Nobody had been able to do anything for the blisters on the middle finger of Ryan's pitching hand during his high school days and in the minors until Mauch suddenly remembered pickle brine.

Velocity Produces Friction

Ryan develops the blisters on his hand because his fastball is released with such a tremendous velocity. He's tried everything, from sandpaper to toughen the skin to a tar compound, kerosene and even fingernail polish. Earlier this year, Mauch tried a solution of alum and alcohol and that didn't work either.

Then Mauch remembered that the Yankees used pickle brine on Hank Borowy's finger because of his blisters and later Tom Morgan got the same treatment. So Gus, who lives in the Bronx, visited the local Daitch Shopwell Market near his apartment and asked the man behind the delicatessen counter for a pint of pickle brine. He'd already been turned down by one store owner who wouldn't sell the brine without the pickle.

"What kind would you like?" asked the man at Daitch, pointing to a row of pickle barrels. "The strongest you got," Mauch told him.

The man reached into the vat of the sourest dill pickles he had, came up with a pint of the brine and the happy Mets trainer made off for Shea Stadium.

He Doesn't Like Pickles

Ryan began dipping his fingers in the pickle brine a fortnight ago. Night and day he dipped them. He never is without his pickle brine. He dips his fingers while sitting in his hotel room, while watching television and before he goes to bed at night. He even dips them in a plastic jar of brine on the dugout bench between innings.

"I can smell the brine when I'm pitching," Ryan said.

However, the Mets have no worry about Nolan putting his finger to his mouth.

"I never really have tried pickles," he said, "but they just look like something I wouldn't like."

Ryan sat in the Mets' clubhouse following his shutout win over the Phillies on May 2 in which he hurled the first seven innings and Ron Taylor finished up.

"Look," he said, displaying his tender finger, "no blisters. That stuff really works."

In that game, Ryan struck out ten and walked seven.

"I was the fastest and the wildest I've been all year," said the rookie from Alvin, Texas. The ten whiffs ran his season total to 36 in 26 innings.

Ryan pitched his first complete game, a 4-1 three-hitter May 7 as he whipped the Cardinals for his third major league victory. No wonder manager Gil Hodges is convinced he has a dilly of a pitcher.

DAD TOOK SPIN AS NOLAN MADE REDS DIZZY

by JACK LANG   **JUNE 1, 1968**

Alvin, Texas, is a town about 20 miles outside of Houston with a population of 12,000. You can probably drive in and out of town and all around it in a half hour, but on any given night when the Mets are playing the Cardinals or the Reds, there's a gent who spends a couple of hours driving around town.

He's Nolan Ryan's father. The reason he gets behind the wheel of his sedan is so that he can pick up broadcasts of the Met games out of St. Louis or Cincinnati—especially when the young strikeout ace is working.

"He can't get the games on the radio in the house," Ryan related, "but he can get them on the car radio. He picked up the game the night I beat the Cardinals and again the night I beat the Reds."

The elder Ryan was so excited he couldn't wait to get on the phone and congratulate his offspring.

His excitement was mild compared with that of the fans in Shea Stadium, where Nolan made local history by setting a club record with 14 strikeouts during a 3-2 win over the Reds.

Fans Rise to Cheer

The 14 Ks eclipsed the old record for a nine-inning game which Tom Seaver and Dick Selma both held at 12. When Ryan accomplished his 12th by fanning the side in the eighth inning, the always hep Shea fans needed no reminder on the message board to tell them what was going on. They were on their feet cheering Ryan as he walked off the field.

With the encouragement he was getting from the 15,671 customers, Ryan hardly could let up in the ninth inning, and he didn't. He added two more by striking out Lee May and Johnny Bench for the record, to give him five batters in a row. Then Tommy Helms—the only man in the starting lineup Ryan failed to fan—lined to left to end the game.

Alex Johnson was Ryan's chief victim. Nolan got the big outfielder three of the four times he faced him.

On the night he set the record—which also gave him a league-leading total of 58 for 44 innings of work—Ryan did not pitch according to form. He did not get most of his victims early as he usually does.

Faster in Twilight

Ryan struck out the first two batters he faced and later admitted that it was the "twilight" that made him appear fast.

"It wasn't quite dark yet at the start of the game so they may have had trouble seeing the ball," he explained.

Usually, Ryan gets five or six strikeouts in the first three innings. In this game, he had only three in the first three. By the fifth, he had eight, but no one was thinking of a record.

After seven innings, he still had only nine, but then came that great finish—five of the last six on swinging strikes.

Relied on Hummer

"I threw nothing but fastballs those last few innings," Ryan said.

In pitching his second complete game, the 21-year-old righthander

---

RYAN'S 14 WHIFFS ONLY 2 OFF ALL-TIME N.Y. MARK

When Nolan Ryan set the Mets' club record with 14 strikeouts, he came within two of tying the best strikeout record of any major league club that ever played in New York.

The most any old Giant or Dodger pitcher fanned in a nine-inning game was 16. Nap Rucker did it for the Dodgers on July 24, 1909, and Christy Mathewson had a similar number for the Giants on October 3, 1904.

The Yankee record is held by Bob Shawkey, who struck out 15 on September 27, 1919.

New York Mets manager Gil Hodges sports a smile, and who wouldn't with a threesome like (left to right) Jerry Koosman, Tom Seaver, and Nolan Ryan, at Shea.

erased all doubts about the strength of his arm.

He threw 146 pitches and was stronger at the end than he was at the start.

Ryan also revealed that the Gus Mauch pickle brine remedy apparently has solved the blister problem on his middle finger.

"It's a little tender now," the pitcher said, "but there's no trace of a blister. I didn't even have to stick my finger in the pickle juice between every inning. I just did it once in this game, after the fifth inning when the finger began to get tender."

In the gay Met clubhouse, the players were kidding Nolan about his hometown.

"Alvin, where's that?" asked Jerry Koosman,

> ## "He could break all the records before he's through."
> ## — Gil Hodges, Mets manager and former teammate of Hall of Fame pitcher Sandy Koufax.

who comes from the thriving metropolis of Appleton, Minnesota. "What kind of town can it be that doesn't have a last name."

Reporters began asking about Alvin and Ryan mentioned the biggest news lately being the erection of a cinema theater.

"We used to have a drive-in, but it got blown down by Hurricane Carla," he said.

"You mean," someone asked, "there's something faster than you in Alvin?"

Gil Hodges, who has played behind such swifties as Sandy Koufax, Rex Barney and Karl Spooner, never ceases to be amazed with Ryan's stuff.

"He could break all the records before he's through," Gil said.

McANDREW AND RYAN TOP QUESTION MARKS ON MET HILL STAFF

by JACK LANG   **FEBRUARY 15, 1969**

NEW YORK—Throughout their off-season in all trade negotiations, Mets general manager Johnny Murphy steadfastly refused to part with either Tom Seaver or Jerry Koosman, insisting repeatedly what he and Gil Hodges both firmly believe:

"Our pitching just isn't that deep that we can afford to give up a Seaver or Koosman," Murphy has said. "Beyond those two, everyone else is a question mark."

Murphy, of course, did not mean to include Don Cardwell or Cal Koonce in the question-mark category. Both are proven pros and both will play a vital role in any success the Mets may have this year.

However, the impression that the Mets are "loaded" with young phenoms is, in Murphy's book, a misconception.

"It's true that we've got some fine young arms," said the smiling Irishman, "but outside of Seaver and Koosman, show me one yet who has proved himself."

To the suggestion that a lot of people would like to have young Jim McAndrew, Murphy counters with the fact that 19 other major league clubs ignored Jim completely in the 1968 draft. McAndrew had posted a 10-8 record with a brilliant 1.47 earned-run average and was advanced to the Jacksonville (International) roster. For a mere $25,000 investment—only $12,500 if they just wanted a look—any major league club could have had McAndrew.

Instead, Jim was bypassed by every big league club and, for a while, ignored even by Jacksonville manager Clyde McCullough. At the start of the 1968 season, Mac had McAndrew in the bullpen. It was farm chief Whitey Herzog who insisted Jim get a shot as a starter, and that was the beginning of the Iowa lad's climb to the majors.

The biggest question mark of all among the young Met pitchers is Nolan Ryan. Last spring, they were wondering whether he was a myth or a marvel. No one knows for sure just yet.

Even though Ryan struck out 56 in his first 44 innings and set a club record with 14 whiffs in one game against the Reds May 1, the slender Texan wound up with a 6-9 record and was unwanted when the Mets offered him in a deal with the Phils in November. "I've had people ask me what happened to Ryan's arm the last half of the season," Murphy pointed out. "They say they didn't see him throw hard. And I didn't see him throw hard either."

Working in regular rotation up to mid-June, Ryan had set that record when suddenly he began getting bombed. He also developed blisters on his fingers when he stopped using the much-publicized pickle brine that had prevented them earlier. Later, he started using sauerkraut juice, but when he finally went to into the Army for two weeks on August 9, he showed nothing upon his return.

Ryan blamed it on not getting enough work and on the layoff caused by his Army stint. Whatever it was, neither Hodges nor Rube Walker used Ryan much in the final month. He didn't win a game after June 23.

"He'll have to show it all over again in spring training," said Herzog. "He's going to get some competition for a job from fellows like Gary Gentry, Jon Matlack and Bob Hendley."

Like Ryan, those three also are question marks at this time in the eyes of the Mets. Gentry and Matlack are unproved kids and Hendley is a veteran attempting to complete a comeback after elbow surgery 15 months ago.

As Murphy said, beyond Seaver and Koosman, the Mets really do not know what they have.

As important to Ryan as his work on the mound was his exercise regimen the days between starts. Here he runs the day after winning Game 3 of the 1969 National League Championship Series.

METS PROGRAM LOTS OF WORK TO GET NOLAN ROLLIN' AGAIN

by JACK LANG   MARCH 8, 1969

ST. PETERSBURG, FLORIDA—A year ago they were calling him Myth or Marvel Ryan. Now that he's no longer a myth, the Mets are counting on Nolan to be the marvel again that he was the first half of last year. They're willing to ignore what happened the last half of the season.

Ryan is the fireballing phenom who had the fantastic minor league record of 449 strikeouts in 291 innings. But most of them were in obscure leagues and recorded in almost total privacy. Gil Hodges and Rube Walker waited most of last spring

before they finally got their first look at Ryan. He quickly convinced them and won a job as a starter.

In fact, Ryan started the fourth game of the season last Easter Sunday, struck out seven of the first ten batters he faced and was well on the way to a 4-0 victory in the seventh inning when one of his famous blisters developed.

Before the season was over, Ryan's strikeouts, his blisters and the pickle brine he used to toughen his fingers were famous enough for national magazines to do spreads on him. Hodges and Walker knew what they had and they brought Ryan along slowly.

Arm is Okay

"There's nothing wrong with his arm," Hodges said after watching Ryan throw recently. "He doesn't have a sore arm, so we don't have to be careful about working him. He just needs work to be a starter again. It's as simple as that."

Hodges and Walker both pointed out that Ryan's frequent military call-ups last year had as much to do as anything else with Nolan's miserable second half. That, plus the fact that Gil and Rube didn't want to hurt the boy's arm.

"If you look it up," Hodges said, "you'll see that in the five months from March to the end of July, Ryan was away a total of ten weekends on reserve duty. The trouble was that he was usually away three or four days when he went and we couldn't work him in regular rotation.

"Then he went into the service in August for two weeks and when he came out, his arm was out of shape. And we weren't gong to push him with the kind of arm he has by rushing him back. There wasn't anything to prove. We knew by then what he could do."

By the time Ryan returned in September, Hodges said, they had an extra starter in Jim McAndrew and there were so many open dates in the schedule that it wasn't worth risking Ryan's arm by forcing him to work

"I thought they could have used me more when I came back," Ryan said, "but I admit I wasn't throwing as hard as I had been before I went away. Maybe my arm wasn't in shape to throw my real good fastball. I know the day in Chicago when I gave up back-to-back homers to Billy Williams and Ernie Banks, both were on fastballs. I guess I wasn't humming it."

Lack of Work Costly

Ryan's fastball, unless it is the super-duper he throws when

he's in shape, is a meatball for most batters. Early in the year, when he was throwing really hard, Ryan gave up only four homers in his first 11 starts.

But then he began missing work because of his Army weekends and he was tagged for six gophers in five games.

Ryan no longer is in a priority military unit and his weekend meetings will be about half of what they were last year. Hodges feels that being around, Ryan will be able to work better in rotation.

"All he needs to do is build up his arm," the manager added. "When we didn't pitch him last year, it was for his own good. He must realize that."

Nolan did work on his own this winter to strengthen his arms. "I built me a chinning bar out back of the house and I chinned every day," the pitcher said. "I also lifted weights. I'm sure they helped strengthen my arms."

Goal is 200 Pounds

Ryan came into the camp well over the 195 he weighed last year, but he's down now to 204. He thinks he'd like to pitch at 200 pounds. But most of all, he'd just like to pitch.

Ryan delivers one of his fireballs after an off-season of conditioning work.

The Sporting News

LAUGHINGSTOCK? METS WIPE GRINS OFF CRITICS' FACES

Ryan Is Mets' Hero in NLCS

by LOWELL REIDENBAUGH   **OCTOBER 18, 1969**

The New York Mets, born to be laughed at, were laughing back. And, oh, how they laughed.

Underdogs...as Usual

In the championship series with the Braves, the Mets again were underdogs—what else—but ig- nored the odds in a three-game sweep that sent experts to their couches.

Casey Stengel called them the "Amazin' Mets."

And in the finale, Nolan Ryan, taking over for Gary Gentry in the third, allowed three hits the rest of the way to pick up the 7-4 victory.

Taking over for Gentry with runners on second

Teammates congratulate Nolan Ryan after he earned a save in Game 3 of the World Series. The teammates, from left to right: Jerry Grote, Wayne Garrett, Tom Seaver, Jerry Koosman, Bud Harrelson and trainer Gus Mauch.

and third and none out in the third inning, Ryan fanned Boyer and got Didier on a fly to left to escape unscathed.

Ryan gave a walk to Carty and a homer to Cepeda in the fifth, but that was all and the Mets made him a winner with three in the sixth. Ryan himself started the rally with the first of his two singles. Garrett's homer netted two runs. Jones' double and Boswell's single produced another.

With the pennant added to their trophies, only one more chapter remains to be written in the tale of the incredible, phenomenal, supernatural Mets in the World Series. Don't bet against it!

THE PLAYOFF
Game 3—1969 NLCS

New York	IP.	H.	R.	ER.	BB.	SO.
Ryan (W)	7	3	2	2	2	7

MET-ICISM WORKS AGAIN

World Series Game 3

by LOWELL REIDENBAUGH   **NOVEMBER 1, 1969**

The Orioles, who were held to two hits in the second game, collected only four safeties off Gentry and Ryan. After Frank Robinson and Boog Powell singled in the fourth, Powell also singled in the sixth and pinch-hitter Clay Dalrymple singled in the ninth as the Orioles loaded the bases with two out.

A walk to Belanger, Dalrymple's hopper through the middle that Al Weis smothered behind second base, and Buford's walk packed the sacks.

On an 0-and-2 count, Ryan switched from his lightning bolts to breaking stuff, and broke a curve over the plate.

Blair was caught looking and Shea Stadium was caught up in one tumultuous roar.

Ryan Decks Powell

Big Boog Powell, batting with one out in the Orioles' eighth, was decked by hard-throwing Nolan Ryan, then bailed out at the plate and looked at a called third strike. Brooks Robinson chased a high fastball and fanned for the third out.

Game 3 —1969 World Series				
New York	IP.	H.	R.	ER.
Gentry (W)	6⅔	3	0	0
Ryan (S)	2⅓	1	0	0

New York Mets rookie righthander Nolan Ryan (left) with teammate Tom Seaver, last season's Rookie of the Year.

Daily News

RYAN "ALL PITCHER" IN ONE-HIT GEM

by JACK LANG **MAY 2, 1970**

NEW YORK—Watching Nolan Ryan that day one could not help but recall Gil Hodges' comment of a few years ago.

"How good is he?" the manager of the Mets said on that occasion after an impressive performance by Ryan.

"Who knows? All I can say is that if he ever puts it all together, he could be one of the greatest pitchers that ever lived."

Ryan still does not fit into that category, but you could not help but feel he was edging a bit closer after a recent performance against the Phillies.

"He put it all together today," said Hodges after Ryan had one-hit the Phillies and set a club record for a nine-inning game with 15 strikeouts.

Actually, Ryan "put it all together" in two halves of the game.

In his first start of the season and in his first appearance on the mound in 16 days, Ryan struck out 14 batters in the first six innings with a fastball that almost no one could touch.

Then, after he admittedly "lost that good zip on my fastball," Ryan, in the words of his manager, was "all pitcher."

Putting It All Together

"He used his change-up and his curveball effectively those last three innings," Hodges said. "He was all pitcher in the latter part of the game. He put it all together this time."

An opposite-field single by leadoff batter Denny Doyle of the Phillies on an 0-and-2 pitch was the only hit Ryan allowed as he pitched the fourth one-hitter in Mets' history.

"It was a bad pitch," the strapping righthander of Alvin, Texas, explained. "I usually like to jam him, but this time I tried to go away and didn't go away enough."

Before that first inning was over, Ryan had loaded the bases with two walks, but he also struck out the side, one of three innings in which he was to accomplish that feat.

Many in the crowd of close to 30,000 at Shea that day were not conscious that Ryan was working on a one-hitter. That was mainly because he constantly was in trouble as a result of six walks in the first five innings, plus two errors. There was always someone on base.

Ryan labored hard and long. By the end of six innings, he had thrown 120 pitches, the normal amount for a nine-inning game. There was much doubt he would finish.

An Occasional Hummer

But, as Hodges said, Ryan became all pitcher in the final three innings, mixing his curvball and his change up effectively and occasionally showing them his fastball to keep the batters honest.

In those final three frames, he struck out only one, but also cut his pitches down to 34 as he faced nine men.

The moment Ryan struck out his 14th batter, he tied the club record, which he shared with Tom Seaver. Then when he fanned Deron Johnson in the eighth, he owned the club record by himself. The only other Met ever to strike out 15 in a game was Jerry Koosman. It took him 15 innings.

Ryan, despite his lack of work, went all the way, and this—more than the one-hitter and the strikeout record—is what he was most proud of.

"It was my first major league shutout," he beamed.

Chagrin showed on the faces of the Phillies just as it must have on managers and players of 10 other clubs in the league.

"Just what the Mets needed," said one Phil dejectedly, "another strong pitcher to go with Seaver and Koosman."

It was indeed discouraging to all other clubs, but most welcome by the Mets, who know they are going to need pitching to win again.

METS TRUMPET LATE ARRIVAL OF RYAN'S EXPRESS

by JACK LANG   **JUNE 12, 1971**

The morning after it happened, the Padres announced that because of a pre-game rock 'n roll concert, there would be no batting practice, no infield practice. Nevertheless, at 10:30 a.m.—2½ hours before the game was to begin—there were three Mets cavorting in the outfield. They were the only three on the field.

Rube Walker, the pitching coach, was hitting fungoes to Tom Seaver and Nolan Ryan. That went on for about 45 minutes.

They still were the only Mets in uniform. The team bus hadn't even arrived yet.

"Rube isn't going to let those two out of his sight," someone remarked.

"Do you blame him?" replied another.

"Look at the numbers on their backs," said one newsman, pointing to the big blue 41 on Seaver's back and the 30 on Ryan's uniform. "What's that add up to?"

"I see what you mean ... 71... they represent 1971."

Seaver and Ryan could very well carry the hopes of the Mets in 1971 on their broad shoulders and with their powerful right arms.

This was the morning after Seaver and Ryan had fanned a record 26 batters in pacing the Mets to a twin win over the Padres. Then they were at the park, cavorting like a couple of rookies eager to pitch again.

If the Padres thought Seaver was fast, they hadn't gotten a glimpse of Ryan.

There's bad news for hitters all over the National League. Ryan's Express has arrived. Like the Long Island Railroad, it's a little late, but it's here.

Ryan followed Seaver's game with a 16-strikeout job in which he squeaked out a 2-1 win.

It was Ryan's career high in strikeouts and raised his season total to 50 in as many innings. What's more, he walked only four (half his usual total) and required only 130 pitches.

"Of those, 110 were fastballs," said Ryan with understandable pride.

No Control Problems

"Did you have trouble controlling the curve? Is that why you went to the fastball so often?" a newsman inquired.

"No," Ryan said in that Texas drawl that is almost boyish at times. "I just had a good fastball so I aired it out."

Ryan has been "airing it out" better than ever this year, which is why he was the Mets' pitching leader with a 6-1 record and ERA leader with 1.08 as May ended.

Nollie doesn't know yet if he's really arrived, but he's beginning to sense it. The Mets are pitching him in regular rotation and not letting those weekend military calls interrupt his work.

Ryan has won all but one of his six starts and in none of them did he allow more than four hits. In fact, in his first 50 innings, the Texas Tornado allowed only 23 hits.

"For the first time in my life," said Ryan, "I can't wait for my next start. The days in between drag out. I never felt exactly that way before."

Adjusting to Big City

Ryan admits he never was happy in New York, but he's beginning to become adjusted to the fast pace. Much of the disenchantment of being in the big city is leaving his lovely wife, Ruth, alone. They are childless and since most other players have families, they do not have much in common.

There have been nothing but raves for Ryan this year. Preston Gomez, the San Diego manager, likened him to Sandy Koufax.

"Every one of his 16 strikeouts was on a swinging third strike," Gomez pointed out. "And half of those were on high pitches...balls. But that's the way Koufax used to get his strikeouts too. The ball comes in and looks like it's going to be a strike and then because of the velocity, it rises, but the batter has to swing anyway."

"He throws harder for one pitch than anyone I've ever seen," said veteran Met infielder Bob Aspromonte.

Ryan has a good curve to go with his hard one, but sometimes he picks the wrong time to use it. Gil Hodges was mildly critical recently when Ryan used it on a 3-and-2 count and walked a man when he was leading by a big score. Eventually, Dan Frisella had to get the last out.

"When you've got that kind of stuff and you're leading big," said the manager, "you don't throw the curve on 3-and-2."

Ryan said he doesn't know for sure yet if he's arrived, but he thinks he's on his way.

"At the end of the season, if I'm 20-5 or 18-6, then I'll say it," he said with an intelligent outlook. "I've had too many ups and downs to be sure I've arrived."

Career at Crossroads

"But I think I've reached a point of maturity. I made up my mind that would be my goal when I started spring training. I felt I was at the point where I must produce or fall by the wayside. I didn't want to stay in baseball if I didn't do it this year."

New York Mets (left to right) Ed Kranepool, Gary Gentry, Tommy Agee and Nolan Ryan celebrate after winning the 1969 World Series against the Baltimore Orioles.

Daily News

NOLAN RYAN'S ABOUT-FACE TOO MUCH FOR GIL TO SOLVE

by JACK LANG　　**SEPTEMBER 4, 1971**

NEW YORK—"I'm sure he's as puzzled as I am," said Nolan Ryan in the Mets' understatement of the season.

Of course manager Gil Hodges is puzzled. He's also confused and disappointed. Ryan has become the enigma of the Mets' pitching staff.

The righthander always has been considered one of the hardest throwers in the game and everyone who saw him agreed that if he ever got in regular rotation, pitching every fourth or fifth day, he couldn't help but be a winner.

But because of weekend military duty, plus two weeks of summer duty every year, Ryan always was thrown off schedule and he never won more than seven games or started more than 19.

This year it was all different. Nollie arranged to do his weekend drills and his two weeks' summer military duty in the New York area. That made him available for the regular rotation and Hodges got him right into the starting rotation in late April.

Just like Tom Seaver, Gary Gentry and Jerry Koosman, he pitched every fifth day and, up until the end of June, it worked out beautifully for the Mets. Ryan had an 8-4 record on June 30 and was right behind Seaver as the club's pitching leader.

Loses Magic Touch

He even had control, which was amazing. There was a stretch in June when he walked no more than two men in each of five games.

But then, just before the All-Star Game, Ryan lost three in a row and in the eight weeks following his eighth victory he won just one game. That was a 20-6 win in Atlanta and he couldn't even finish that one.

You talk to Rube Walker, the pitching coach, and to Hodges, the manager, and they can't figure it.

"It's nothing physical," said Walker. "If he were hurting or something, we could understand it. But he's fine. There's nothing wrong with his arm. It's just that he can't get the ball over the plate."

"We knew what his problems were in the past," added Hodges. "But he doesn't have those troubles this year. There's been nothing to interrupt his schedule. We thought the way he started out the season that this year would be the big one. He's already won more games than ever before and he did that in half a season."

A Trip to the Bullpen

Hodges decided, following Ryan's quick fadeout in Los Angeles in his most recent start, that perhaps a few days in the bullpen might help.

"I'll just take him out of the rotation for a few games and see what happens," the manager said. He didn't anticipate it would solve the problem, but that's because no one can figure the Ryan riddle.

Ryan admits that he's completely befuddled by what's happened to him this year.

"I couldn't ask for a better break," he conceded. "They've given me every opportunity. I always wanted to start every fourth or fifth day and I have. I'm as puzzled as everyone else."

Ryan already has made more starts and pitched more innings than any other year in his career. He also has won more games than ever before...two more to be exact.

But, like Hodges said, he won all but one of those in the first half of the season when he was rolling.

METS SWAP RYAN? "NO WAY," SAYS GIL

by JACK LANG **OCTOBER 9, 1971**

Any speculation that the Mets were about ready to give up on Nolan Ryan was quickly dismissed by manager Gil Hodges even before the hard-throwing righthander ended a seven-week drought with a victory over the Cubs.

"Oh, no," said the manager, suggesting genuine surprise that anyone would even entertain such a thought. "We never have given any consideration to trading Nolan Ryan.

"You cannot give up easily on a boy who has as much talent as he has. You would hate to give up on him and then see him develop into what he can be with some other club."

No one would have given any thought to trading Ryan the way he was pitching earlier this year. He was rolling along with an 8-4 record at the end of June and pitching in regular rotation for the first time in his career.

But then Nolan went into a tailspin and lost nine of his next 10 decisions before finally beating the Cubs in the final game the Mets played in Chicago this season.

Ryan has been a complete puzzle to the Mets and to pitching coach Rube Walker. His inability to control his great stuff often has had outsiders wondering if it was worth being so pa-tient. After all, this is his fourth season with the Mets and, despite flashes of brilliance, he has never won more than seven games before this season.

Ready for Peak Year

And this was the season Ryan's Express was finally going to arrive. All the pieces were fitting into place. He had worked out his military commitments so he needn't be away four days every month and he served his summer duty in New York.

The way the season began, Ryan seemed sure of winning 15 or maybe even 20 games. He had eight victories after a dozen starts and would get another 20 starts before it was over.

Then something happened. The control that Ryan discovered in June deserted him in July, August and the first half of September.

Once again he was the wild man of old, hitting batters, walking batters, making wild pitches. It got so they'd start guessing in the press box how long Ryan would last.

To the everlasting credit of Hodges and Walker, they have not given up on Ryan. He has continued to start. Maybe not every fifth day, but he has continued to start.

"It shows they have some confidence in me,"

SCHEFFING DOUBTS METS WILL DROP BLOCKBUSTER

By Jack Lang
December 4, 1971

General manager Bob Scheffing still has hopes of making a deal for the slugger the Mets need, but he doesn't think it's going to be the blockbuster the fans are expecting.

On the eve of the winter meetings, Scheffing conceded that the Mets have talked to every club in the majors and then quickly ruled out a dozen of them.

"I'm pretty sure we won't do any business with an American League club," he confided. "Something could open up again in Phoenix, but I doubt it."

Another point Scheffing conceded was that the Mets are not going to give up a lot of players just to get one.

Allen Deal Unlikely

Scheffing doubted that Richie Allen would be available from the Dodgers. "They seem pretty happy with him," he opined.

The one interesting point mentioned by Scheffing was that while most clubs ask for Gary Gentry, no one asks for Nolan Ryan anymore.

"When his name does come up they want him as a throw-in," Scheffing said with a laugh.

said Ryan before the game in Chicago when he got off the spot.

"At least that's gratifying. I have not done much to earn it, but they are not giving up on me."

Ryan and his lovely wife, Ruth, who is expecting their first child later this year, are a couple of lost kids in the big city. They are country folk and they don't cotton to the fast life in New York. Ryan himself has expressed the opinion more than once that perhaps a change of scenery would be best for him.

But winning, of course, can produce a lot of comfort. After Ryan won his 10th game with the decision over the Cubs, he was a much more relaxed man.

"I had difficulty controlling the fastball," he admitted after hitting the first batter he faced and walking the next two.

"But then I went to more breaking stuff, especially the slow curve," he pointed out, "and I was able to handle them."

The Cubs got seven hits off Ryan on a day when he wasn't throwing his blazer. And two of the four runs were unearned.

Potential Is Exciting

It's no wonder the Mets aren't about to give up on a boy with that kind of talent. Especially since Jerry Koosman continues to have so much trouble regaining his fastball.

The Mets can't go to spring training next year counting on Kooz to be a big winner. But maybe they can count on Ryan.

METS REGARD FREGOSI AS CURE TO 10-YEAR HOT SACK ANEMIA

by JACK LANG **DECEMBER 25, 1971**

NEW YORK—"We're getting a professional hitter...a bear-down type of guy...a hustling ballplayer. At least he was when I was over in that league."

Thus did manager Gil Hodges view the deal that brought Jim Fregosi to the Mets for Nolan Ryan and minor leaguers Don Rose, Leroy Stanton and Frank Estrada.

Fregosi, for an infielder, always has been a solid RBI man. He had his greatest year in 1970 when he slammed 22 homers, drove in 82 runs and batted .278.

Mets Searched in Vain

Hodges admits that he does not expect that kind of year out of Fregosi but anything close will be a blessing for the Mets, who have been searching for a third baseman since 1962—the year of their birth.

Hodges said he hated to let Nolan Ryan go because he still feels the big righthander from Texas has the potential to become a star.

"Whether or if or how he's going to do it, I don't know," said the Mets' manager. "But he's got ability."

Regarding the deal in which the Mets gave up four players to get Fregosi, Gil offered the opinion that the Mets' roster was not disturbed. "It amounts to a Ryan-for-Fregosi deal as far as our roster is concerned," Hodges opined.

3 CHAPTER

THE EXPRESS ARRIVES

I n 1972 and 1973, Nolan Ryan began to emerge as a legitimate major-league star. In 1972, he began re-writing the Angels' record books, then moved on to setting new American League records, a trend that continued throughout the rest of his career. He pitched the first two of his no-hitters in 1973, on May 15 against the Royals and on July 15 against the Tigers, and missed two more by the slimmest of margins. That same season, he struck out 383 batters, breaking Sandy Koufax's record of 382 in 1965. Despite his numerous accomplishments, he placed second to Jim Palmer in the voting for the Cy Young Award. He did, however, pick up the Helms Award for Southern California's athlete of the year.

RYAN'S SNAKE OIL BLESSING TO ANGELS

by DICK MILLER   **JULY 8, 1972**

ANAHEIM—Maybe the American Medical Association should throw away its needles and buy shotguns.

Dr. Snake Oil has become the personal physician of the Angels' pitching staff.

He's listed on the roster as Nolan Ryan. In the California clubhouse, however, he's addressed as Dr. Snake Oil, the healer who cured Clyde Wright's painful shoulder and his own aching right elbow.

Ryan did it with oil from rattlesnakes. Honest!

A testimonial was offered by Wright, who had to miss two turns and was advised he would have to pitch with pain all season. But the pain turned out to be to American League hitters after Ryan loaned him a bottle of his secret cureall, which actually is an ancient remedy.

"Dr. Snake Oil did it," said the Anaheim Hill Billy. "My shoulder hasn't hurt me since he gave it to me."

The record backs up the testimonial. Through games of June 23, Wright had a 7-3 record and an ERA of 2.26. His earned-run mark was more than half a run a game under his figure of 1970 when Wright won 22 games and was *The Sporting News'* selection as the Comeback Player of the Year.

Ryan discovered the cure-all last winter.

"I didn't believe it myself until I went hunting with an old man back home," the pitcher revealed.

"He was all crippled up with arthritis.

"He shot a rattler and three days later he was better.

"A few weeks after my wife had the baby, her back hurt her so much she couldn't pick the baby up. She tried it and it's been all right ever since."

Outside of carefully, how does one go about striking oil in a rattlesnake?

"You gut him," said Ryan, "and boil the oil. You'd be surprised how much oil you get out of a three- or four-year-old rattler."

The snake oil is rubbed into the sore joint and a heating pad applied.

> **"I didn't believe it myself until I went hunting with an old man back home. He was all crippled up with arthritis. He shot a rattler and three days later he was better."**

It's helped Ryan's own tender elbow.

The righthander had the lowest ERA of his career (3.04) after 14 games and had struck out 81 batters in 80 innings.

Nolan may lead the world in exotic cures. Remember the Mets' nationwide search for pickle brine to cure blisters on his pitching hand?

Don't be surprised someday if he visits an acupuncture specialist who prescribes a diet of organic herbs imported from a monastery in Tibet.

But, until then, rattlesnakes may go on the endangered species list.

ANGEL RECORDS FALL ON RYAN EXPRESSWAY

by DICK MILLER   **JULY 22, 1972**

ANAHEIM—Rudy May calls him "Greatness."

"He's faster than instant coffee, wall-to-wall heat," said Oakland's Reggie Jackson.

Clyde Wright has another name for Nolan Ryan, "Dr. Snake Oil."

But if you want to know the truth, the pitcher should be called Clifford Irving. He's spending the season rewriting two books—the American League and Angels' record books.

On July 9, as he was pitching a one-hitter while blanking the Red Sox, 3-0, Nolan struck out 16 batters, the second time he accomplished the feat this season. He took over the A.L. strikeout lead from Mickey Lolich with 138.

In whiffing 16 Oakland batsmen July 1, Ryan had broken the Angels' club record held jointly by Cy Young Award winner Dean Chance and Jorge Rubio.

In the July 9 game, Carl Yastrzemski got the lone hit, a one-out solid single in the first inning. After that, Ryan fanned the next eight men for an American League record. The three men he whiffed in the second inning went down on nine straight pitches to equal a major league mark, the 15th time it had been done.

For Ryan, this was the second time he had whiffed three men on nine successive pitches.

Following Yaz' single, the Angels' fireballer retired the next 26 men in order.

And in pitching his second straight shutout, Nolan made it five consecutive complete-game victories, another Angels' all-time high.

With 47 strikeouts in four games and 57 in five games, Ryan had eclipsed two more Chance marks.

That's why teammate May, who has the adjoining locker to Ryan's at Anaheim Stadium, said admiringly after the 16-strikeout performances, "Greatness, you are too much."

In his last five starts, Ryan allowed only 18 hits across 45 innings, leading Oakland's Jackson, the American League home-run leader, to say:

"He's the only man in baseball I'm afraid of. He throws it in my power zone and I can't get the bat around fast enough. If one ever gets away from him, he will kill someone."

Jackson's theory drew support from another renowned home-run hitter, Minnesota's Harmon Killebrew.

"If he ever hits me with a fastball, I'll have him arrested for manslaughter," said the Killer.

John Roseboro, who made a living catching the fastballs of Sandy Koufax and Don Drysdale, had this to add:

"I've only caught Ryan on the sidelines," the bullpen coach said, "so I can't compare his fastball to Sandy's. But he scares batters in a manner that Sandy didn't simply because Koufax never threw close to a batter."

Like Koufax, Ryan appears to have found himself as a pitcher after years of struggling.

Matched against a revived Milwaukee club on July 5, one that had won nine of its last 13 games, Ryan discovered in the bullpen the heat was missing from his fastball and his curve was a memory.

So he shut out the Brewers on four hits while striking out eight.

Through July 9, Ryan already had passed his career high in wins (11) while leading the staff in complete games (9), innings (125), strikeouts (138) and ERA (2.30).

The arrival of the Ryan Express is three years ahead of the schedule of Koufax.

It also presents a dilemma for Earl Weaver, manager of the American League team in the All-Star Game July 25 at Atlanta. Since every team must be represented by at least one player and it appears likely no California regular will be voted into the contest, the Baltimore skipper probably will pick an Angel pitcher, Ryan or Clyde Wright.

Asked if he would like to be picked on the team, Ryan uncorked a surprising pitch:

"Not especially," he admitted. "I enjoy being with my family. But if I'm picked I'll go."

ONLY SAM, SANDY TOP RYAN'S K PACE

by DICK MILLER

OCTOBER 14, 1972

ANAHEIM—It was last December, a few days after the Angels' new general manager, Harry Dalton, had traded shortstop Jim Fregosi to the Mets for pitcher Nolan Ryan and three other players.

"How do you like the deal?" the USC basketball broadcaster asked a reporter on a halftime interview.

"Really great," the reporter replied sarcastically. "With Wright, Messersmith, and May, the Angels need another pitcher with potential like Howard Hughes needs a publicity agent."

A few weeks into the season, Fregosi was batting cleanup on a Met team that was leading the National League East. Ryan was on the sidelines with a pulled groin muscle. Outfielder Lee Stanton was on the bench, a huge disappointment.

Pitcher Don Rose and catcher Francisco Estrada were in the minors.

And Dalton was under fire as the Angels got off to the slowest start in their history.

Now it is six months later and Dalton is being hailed as a genius. Bothered by two major injuries, Fregosi spent most of the second half on the bench as the Mets floundered.

Stanton battled his way back into Rookie of the Year contention while finishing second on the club in home runs and fourth in RBIs.

Ryan, the man they call The Express, might have won a Cy Young Award with a team that could produce runs.

"He would have won 26 or 27 games if we could have gotten him three runs a game," said manager Del Rice. At the time, The Express had 18 victories with two starts remaining.

Upon joining the California Angels, Ryan began his pursuit of team and league records.

AP/Wide World Photos

He has struck out 10 or more batters in 15 games. The Express fanned the side 20 times—the equivalent of two full games with a couple of innings left over. He struck out the side on nine pitches against Boston, setting an American League record with eight consecutive strikeouts in that game.

Ironically, the same Mets who traded Ryan are hopeful of obtaining a pitcher from the Angels this winter.

You wonder what kind of excitement Ryan would have generated at Shea Stadium this summer if he was still wearing a Mets uniform.

The crowds were under 5,000 at Anaheim Stadium as Ryan's fastball struck out batters at a pace that threatened the modern baseball record.

Through September 28, he had fanned 302 in 266 innings for a nine-inning average of 10.22. Only Sudden Sam McDowell (10.71 in 1965) and Sandy Koufax (10.23 the same year) had a greater strikeout ratio since the turn of the century.

At the same time, Ryan was battling Philadelphia's Steve Carlton for the major league leadership in strikeouts.

Ryan was the easy shutout leader in the American League—if you count the number of times the Angels were blanked while he was working.

Of his 15 defeats, six were via the shutout route, twice by Detroit (Lolich each time) and Chicago (Wood and Bahnsen), and once each by Kansas City (Nelson) and Texas (Gogolewski).

In absorbing the six losses, Ryan gave up 10 runs—only six earned—in 46 innings for an ERA of 1.17.

The numbers tell how overpowering the righthander has been in 1972. He has struck out 10 or more batters in 15 games. The Express fanned the side 20 times—the equivalent of two full games with a couple of innings left over.

He struck out the side on nine pitches against Boston, setting an American League record with eight consecutive strikeouts in that game.

And he set a club record with three consecutive shutouts.

That's why Harry Dalton will have the "Not For Sale" sign up at the winter meetings.

WHIFF ARTISTS

SO	Pitcher	Year	IP	9-Inn. Avg.
382	Koufax	1965	336	10.23
349	Waddell	1904	384	8.20
348	Feller	1946	372	8.42
325	McDowell	1965	273	10.71
317	Koufax	1967	323	8.83
313	Johnson	1910	374	7.53
308	Lolich	1971	376	7.37
306	Koufax	1963	311	8.86
304	McDowell	1970	305	8.97
303	Carlton	1972	337	8.09
303	Johnson	1912	368	7.41
302	RYAN	1967	266	10.22
301	Blue	1971	312	8.68
301	Waddell	1903	323	8.39

ANGEL RYAN FOREMOST FIEND TO A.L. HITTERS

by DICK MILLER **DECEMBER 30, 1972**

ANAHEIM—"Everything You Always Wanted To Know About Pitching . . . But Didn't Know Who to Ask."

(Q) Who is "the toughest-to-hit" pitcher in the American League?

(A) Nolan Ryan.

(Q) If a pitcher leads a league in strikeouts, about how many pitches will he have to throw during the season?

(A) Nolan Ryan threw 4,608 pitches last season, 2,822 of them strikes.

(Q) By contrast, how many pitches will a good control pitcher throw if he takes his turn every fourth day?

(A) Clyde Wright required only 3,229 pitches, 1,961 of them in the strike zone or swung at.

(Q) Which was the hardest pitching staff in the American League to get a hit off last season?

(A) California's, followed by Baltimore, Oakland and Minnesota.

The above answers were supplied by two unique statistical teams. Coach Jimmie Reese kept track of every pitch made by the California staff last season. If you want to win a trivia test, ask someone to guess, within 2,000, how many pitches a staff will make during a season (20,447 by the Angels).

Of that total, 12,506 were strikes and 7,941 were balls.

The other survey was compiled by the firm of George Lederer, George Goodale and Ed Munson, the Angels' public relations staff. It showed that Ryan held opposing batters to a .170 average, 19 percentage points ahead of runner-up Jim (Catfish) Hunter of Oakland. The Angels' staff limited opponents to a .222 average, shading the Orioles (.224) and A's (.226).

Ryan's unique title was determined among qualifiers for the ERA title, based on 156 innings or more of work.

In 284 innings, the Ryan Express allowed only 166 hits for 973 official at-bats. He was most effective against the Tigers, holding the East Division champions to a .142 average. Against all other pitchers, the Tigers batted .239.

Only New York (.400) and Cleveland batters (.222) were able to break the .200 barrier against Ryan. He worked only 3⅓ innings against the Yankees.

THE YARDSTICK

Following are 1972 statistics featuring team performances against the top A.L. pitchers and, below, Nolan Ryan's record.

BATTING AVERAGES VS. TOP A.L. PITCHERS

	AB.	H.	PCT.
NOLAN RYAN, CALIFORNIA	973	166	.170
Catfish Hunter, Oakland	1,056	200	.189
Roger Nelson, Kansas City	612	120	.196
Luis Tiant, Boston	633	128	.202
Gaylord Perry, Cleveland	1,235	253	.205
Jim Palmer, Baltimore	1,009	219	.217
Mike Cuellar, Baltimore	896	197	.220
Pat Dobson, Baltimore	980	220	.224
Ray Corbin, Minnesota	587	135	.230
Mickey Lolich, Detroit	1,205	282	.234
John Odom, Oakland	701	164	.234
Wilbur Wood, Chicago	1,384	325	.235
Ken Holtzman, Oakland	981	232	.236
Steve Kline, New York	887	210	.237
Mike Paul, Texas	605	149	.246

BATTING AVERAGES VS. NOLAN RYAN

	AB.	H.	PCT.	W-L
Detroit	106	15	.142	2-2
Kansas City	97	14	.144	2-1
Baltimore	33	5	.152	1-1
Milwaukee	90	14	.156	2-1
Texas	99	16	.162	2-2
Oakland	152	25	.164	3-3
Boston	77	13	.169	1-1
Chicago	113	20	.177	1-3
Minnesota	110	20	.182	3-1
Cleveland	81	18	.222	2-0
New York	15	6	.400	0-1
Totals	973	166	.170	19-16

ANGELS POINT RYAN EXPRESS TOWARD 30 WINS

by DICK MILLER   **MARCH 31, 1973**

PALM SPRINGS—Nolan Ryan, who conceded, "There was more excitement in the parking lots at Mets games than at Anaheim Stadium last year," could change all that by becoming the third pitcher since the early 1930s to win 30 games.

He probably will get enough starts to have a shot at that figure, Bobby Winkles revealed after the strikeout king opened the exhibition season with three shutout innings against the Cubs.

The rookie manager said he would use only a three-man rotation in the final month of the season.

"I guess I'm different than most managers that way," said Winkles.

At the same time, he revealed he would also adopt the White Sox' three-man rotation "if any of the starters are struggling the first month and have to go to the bullpen to straighten out."

That could give Ryan, Clyde Wright and Rudy May between eight and 10 extra starts.

The way he performed in the opener, Ryan may not need the extra work to reach the magic 30. He faced only nine Cubs in his first '73 outing. Last spring, he averaged two walks an inning and two to three hit batters a game.

Against the same Cubs in his debut a year ago, the Ryan Express walked five, yielded four hits and was battered for five runs in three innings.

Ryan figures to get 42 starts this season. He had 39 in '72, skipping two turns with a leg injury and missing one start because of the players' strike.

Bill Singer figures to be the fourth man in the Angels' rotation. He was battered for eight hits and four runs in his first three innings of work as an Angel. But Singer's American League baptism was no rougher than Ryan's last season.

You know what happened to Nolan. He went on to lead the universe with 329 strikeouts and tied for the major league lead with nine shutouts.

If the Angels had given him three runs a game, Ryan would have finished with a 26-10 record.

Jimmie Reese's pitching chart told the difference between the confident Ryan of today and the Singer who is struggling to find himself.

Ryan made 38 pitches, 21 of them strikes. In the same number of innings, Singer threw 61 times trying to find the higher American League strike zone.

Pitching coach Tom Morgan thinks the former Dodger will find himself. "I'd say he threw 20 pitches very well," said the man who pointed Ryan and Rudy May to the winner's circle.

Ryan thinks the seven-player deal with the Dodgers turned the Californians into contenders.

"I really feel that way," Nolan said. "There's a lot of ifs with injuries, but now we have the hitting. It would be tough for me to win 30, but I don't have to win 30 for us to win a pennant. I think we'll draw a million people this year."

He'd like the feeling of working before big crowds again.

"I like to pitch before big crowds," admitted the man who put 3,000 extra people in the park every game last year. "It was tough adjusting to the crowds in Anaheim. There was more enthusiasm in the parking lots at Mets games.

"That's what is good about New York. They appreciate good baseball. I can't think of anything better than appearing before a big crowd. I can remember standing in the outfield and watching the people get off the subway. It was wall-to-wall people. They had people standing 600 feet behind the right field fence."

RYAN'S NO-NO SPIKES ROYALS

by DICK MILLER

JUNE 2, 1973

ANAHEIM—When it comes to thank-yous for no-hitters, it is customary for the pitchers to present posies to their catchers, the teammates who made the good defensive plays and, of course, the men who drove in the runs.

Nolan Ryan thanked catcher Jeff Torborg, shortstop Rudy Meoli and outfielder Ken Berry, along with muscleman Bob Oliver, for their parts in his 3-0 no-hitter at Kansas City May 15.

But he also was ready to thank Jack McKeon, the manager of the Royals. McKeon played the game under protest and tried to upset the Angels' pitcher with appeals that he was pitching illegally.

"I want to thank Jack," Ryan said the day after striking out 12 and walking three. "Jack did me a favor causing all that commotion. When I bring my foot off the rubber (the basis of McKeon's appeal), it usually means that I'm rocking back too far and I get wild, high.

"He didn't shake me up, he settled me down. I cut my back stride and everything turned out just fine."

McKeon withdrew his protest the next day, which was just as well. Can you imagine American League President Joe Cronin throwing out a no-hitter on a technicality?

In his last start before the no-hitter, Ryan lasted one out and 17 pitches against the White Sox. In the game before that, he walked seven Orioles in a 5-0 loss.

It was about half an hour before game time when Ryan and Bobby Valentine took the long walk down the tunnel that leads from the visitors' clubhouse at Royals Stadium to the field.

Neither had seen much light at the end of the tunnel recently as they took the long walk. Valentine, the early-season batting leader, was 0-for-26. Condemned men at Alcatraz used to take shorter walks.

Ryan finally broke the silence. "Why don't we break out of our slumps tonight?" asked the conductor of the Ryan Express.

Valentine broke his with an infield hit. Ryan did a little better with his no-hitter, an awesome performance that saw him highball his way to at least one strikeout in every inning except the fifth.

What was the third no-hitter in California history worth? Ryan says he doesn't care. General manager Harry Dalton says he won't know until the end of the season.

"They didn't take any of my money away when I was pitching poorly," said the pitcher. "We'll take a look at it at the end of the season," said the general manager.

Ryan used a mixture of about 70 percent

LONG SHOT?
by Melvin Durslag
June 9, 1973

LOS ANGELES—You note first that since each of the 24 teams in the major leagues plays 162 games, a total of 3,888 opportunities a year is offered for a no-hitter.

Over the last 71 years, an average of two-a-season has been achieved.

So what Las Vegas is dealing with is roughly a 2,000-to-1 shot, which isn't exactly odds-on, but not as long, say, as the price on bowling a 300 game, for which the chances are 6,000-to-1.

And when you talk about a hole-in-one on a normal par 3, a pricemaker will give you 10,000-to-1 from now until Halloween.

This isn't to minimize what Nolan Ryan of the Angels did the other evening. He pitched a no-hitter against Kansas City, marking the 74th time this has been done since the start of the American League in 1901.

In the National League, pitchers have done it 99 times since 1876.

It isn't as hard as striking out 18, or, for that matter fanning eight batters in a row.

fastballs to curves. He threw 80 strikes and 52 balls. The fastballs came close to breaking the sound barrier.

"He was throwing the ball harder than any man I ever saw in my life," said John Mayberry, the American League's RBI leader. "If they had a higher league," said Hal McRae, "he could be in it. As a matter of fact, he could be it."

Calmest man in the park probably was Torborg, who caught his third no-hitter. With the Dodgers, he also handled Sandy Koufax's perfect game against the Cubs in 1965 and Bill Singer's no-hitter against the Phillies in 1970. Since Torborg has appeared in only 374 major league games, it works out to about one no-hitter a year over a 162-game schedule.

And you thought there were no new statistics in baseball.

Jeff wasn't nervous as the end drew near.

"Nolan has thrown this hard before," said the catcher. "But you get to the point where it's humanly impossible to throw any harder. He was very fast, really great, and his curve was excellent, too.

"He really had great stuff," continued Torborg, "right there with Koufax and Singer."

It was evident early that this was one of those times The Express was on the right track, one that some say will some day lead to Cooperstown. He struck out the side in the first inning, one batter in the second, and a pair of Royals in the third. He added one more in the fourth, sixth, seventh, eighth and ninth innings.

Ryan became the first righthander in the Angels' 13-year history to throw a no-hitter. Bo Belinsky recorded the first against the Red Sox in 1962 and another southpaw, Clyde Wright, pitched one against the Athletics in 1970.

For years, people have said that Ryan, like Koufax, could pitch an annual no-hitter. The 26-year-old Ryan never believed that talk.

"I never honestly felt I was the type of pitcher to pitch a no-hitter," Ryan said standing next to his locker.

"My curveball isn't overpowering and after you've gone through the lineup once or twice, the hitters can get on the fastball better. A lot of that's timing. I don't have the type of fastball that really moves. A lot of guys have that explosive type of fastball that really moves.

"Also, I jam the hitters a lot, so the really strong guys can just bloop the ball over the infield for singles."

MAY 15, 1973
California 3, Kansas City 0

CALIFORNIA	ab	r	h	bi	KANSAS CITY	ab	r	h	bi
Pinson 1f	5	1	2	0	Patek ss	4	0	0	0
Alomar 2b	4	0	0	0	Hovley rf	3	0	0	0
Valentine cf	4	0	1	0	Otis cf	4	0	0	0
Robinson dh	3	1	1	0	Mayberry 1b	3	0	0	0
Oliver rf	4	1	2	2	Rojas 2b	3	0	0	0
Berry rf	0	0	0	0	Kirkpatrick dh-c	3	0	0	0
Gallagher 3b	4	0	2	1	Piniella 1f	3	0	0	0
Spencer 1b	4	0	1	0	Schaal 3b	2	0	0	0
Meoli ss	4	0	1	0	Taylor c	1	0	0	0
Torborg c	4	0	1	0	Hopkins ph	1	0	0	0
TOTALS	36	3	11	3		27	0	0	0

California   2 0 0   0 0 1   0 0 0—3
Kansas City   0 0 0   0 0 0   0 0 0—0

DP—Kansas City 1. LOB—California 8, Kansas City 3. HR—Oliver (4). SB—Hovley. S—Alomar.

CALIFORNIA	IP	H	R	ER	BB	SO
Ryan (W 5-3)	9	0	0	0	3	12

KANSAS CITY						
Dal Canton (L 2-2)	5⅔	8	3	3	1	0
Garber	3⅓	3	0	0	0	0

RYAN'S SMOKE SENDS TIGERS INTO NO-HIT BLIND

by DICK MILLER   JULY 28, 1973

DETROIT—The Surgeon General of the United States should do something about Nolan Ryan's fastball.

A notice similar to that appearing on cigarette packages would contain this warning:

"Nolan Ryan's smoke is dangerous to a batter's health. It causes shortness of breath and should be avoided."

Detroit's Tigers couldn't avoid the smoke from Ryan's fastball on July 15 and became The Express' second no-hit victim. Exactly two months after the righthander shut out the Royals at Kansas City, Ryan became the fifth pitcher in major league history to record two no-hitters in a single season.

He struck out 17 at Tiger Stadium while walking four. There were no errors behind him in the 6-0 victory before an awe-struck audience of 41,411.

The Tigers couldn't hit Ryan with a paddle. Really. Norm Cash carried one to the plate in the fifth inning. Plate umpire Ron Luciano, who developed tendinitis raising his right arm on third strikes, threw the paddle out of the game.

Ryan threw 126 pitches. Jimmie Reese's pitching chart showed 81 strikes and 45 balls.

Ryan's fastballs were easy to detect on television. They were the ones with vapor trails.

After four straight losses and five in six games, Angel skipper Bobby Winkles awoke Sunday morning with a slight headache.

Ryan provided fast, fast relief. The little white blurs Tiger batters were seeing weren't aspirin tablets.

They were Bufferin. You know, twice as fast as aspirin.

It was Angel catcher Art Kusnyer who required Bufferin after the game. The first finger on his left hand was beginning to turn purple. "It's a bone bruise," the seldom-used receiver analyzed.

"I've never had anything like it before. But Nollie was throwing so hard. . ."

He was throwing so hard he had 16 strikeouts at the end of seven innings. Bob Feller's American League record of 18 and the major league standard of 19 held by Tom Seaver and Steve Carlton were within easy reach.

But Ryan's arm stiffened up while his teammates took 30 minutes to bat around for five runs in the eighth inning.

A two-run single by Al Gallagher and a pinch two-run hit by Winston Llenas took the pressure off a 1-0 game.

The no-hitter was the fourth in the Angels' 13-year history. Bo Belinsky (against Baltimore) and Clyde Wright (vs. Oakland) preceded Ryan's no-no extravaganza at Kansas City.

The no-hitter caught Ryan by surprise. He was prepared only for a shutout.

"When I woke up this morning I was 'up' for the game," Ryan said afterward. "I decided to shut them out. I needed it (his record is only 11-11 despite the two no-hitters) and the team needed it the way we were going.

"The umpire (Luciano) was very, very good. He didn't have many borderline calls and that made it easier for him."

Ryan was disappointed he didn't get 20 strikeouts.

"I really wanted the strikeout record," he confessed. "I honestly believe it will be easier for me to strike out 20 than pitch another no-hitter."

That news should delight American League hitters. With 220 strikeouts, the Ryan Express already is highballing down the track at a pace that will make him the first pitcher in baseball history to strike out 400 batters in a season.

Ryan thought he had better stuff than against Kansas City.

"I was more pleased with this one," said Ryan. "Beating a veteran ball club and in this park means more," he added.

Ancient Tiger Stadium, perhaps the best park for hitters in baseball, had not been the scene of a no-hitter in 21 years until Kansas City's Steve Busby blanked the Detroiters earlier this season.

AP/Wide World Photos

Ryan fires it home during his second no-hitter, July 15, 1973, against the Tigers in Detroit.

JULY 15, 1973
California 6, Detroit 0

CALIFORNIA	ab	r	h	bi	KANSAS CITY	ab	r	h	bi
Alomar 2b	5	0	2	0	Northrup 1f	4	0	0	0
Pinson rf	4	0	0	1	Stanley cf	3	0	0	0
McCraw 1f	2	0	0	0	Brown dh	2	0	0	0
Llenas ph	1	0	1	2	Cash 1b	4	0	0	0
Stanton 1f	0	1	0	0	Sims c	3	0	0	0
Epstein 1b	3	1	1	0	McAuliffe 2b	3	0	0	0
Oliver dh	3	1	1	1	Sharon rf	2	0	0	0
Berry cf	3	0	0	0	Rodriguez 3b	3	0	0	0
Gallagher 3b	4	0	2	2	Brinkman ss	3	0	0	0
Meoli ss	4	1	1	0					
Kusnyer c	3	2	1	0					
TOTALS	32	6	9	6		27	0	0	0

```
California    0 0 1    0 0 0    0 5 0—6
Detroit       0 0 0    0 0 0    0 0 0—0
```

DP—Detroit 2. LOB—California 5, Kansas City 4. 2B—Epstein, Meoli. SF—Pinson

CALIFORNIA	IP	H	R	ER	BB	SO
Ryan (W 11-11)	9	0	0	0	4	17

DETROIT	IP	H	R	ER	BB	SO
J. Perry (L 9-9)	7⅓	5	3	3	3	2
Scherman	⅓	0	0	0	0	0
B. Miller	0	2	3	3	1	0
Farmer	1⅓	2	0	0	1	0

A THIRD NO-HITTER IN 1973? NOLAN MIGHT DO IT

by DICK MILLER **AUGUST 11, 1973**

ANAHEIM—Nolan Ryan insists he doesn't believe in dreams or premonitions.

But he was an 11- or 12-year-old Little Leaguer when he first knew he would become a major-league player.

In his final two starts before the All-Star break, the conductor of Ryan's Express threw a no-hitter against Detroit and what easily could have been another historic no-hitter against Baltimore.

A single by Mark Belanger in the eighth inning July 19 prevented Ryan from matching Johnny Vander Meer's consecutive no-hitters. The Orioles went on to win the game in the 11th inning, with Ryan yielding three hits.

From Las Vegas, Jimmy (The Greek) Snyder reported the odds are 70 to 1 that Ryan will become the first pitcher in major league history to throw three no-hitters in a single season.

Ryan, who threw a no-no at Kansas City May 15, likes the odds.

"Personally," he confessed, "I think I have a good chance of throwing another one if I keep my stuff and have some luck."

The final two months of the season may be without parallel for baseball fans. While Henry Aaron chases the ghost of Babe Ruth in the National League, Ryan is striking out batters at a faster pace than did the living legend, Sandy Koufax.

At his present pace, Ryan not only will surpass Koufax's record 382 strikeouts of 1965, but could break the 400 barrier.

He talked about dreams and premonitions one night at Anaheim Stadium as he went through his nightly yoga and stretching exercises. He was actually standing on his head, his feet braced against the left field wall at Anaheim Stadium, when he said:

"I really had no premonition I was going to throw the no-hitter at Detroit. I don't believe in premonitions. The only premonition I ever had was when I was in Little League. We had lost a bi-district tournament and were lined up on the field afterward for ceremonies.

"We were feeling pretty low. Some former major leaguer, and I can't remember his name, was passing out the awards. He said, 'One of you boys is going to be a major league player some day.'

"I thought at the time I would be that boy."

At 26, Ryan remains, basically, the same country boy from Alvin, Texas, who found it hard to adjust to life in New York.

Some pitchers put on a Dracula act before they start a game. They don't want to talk to anyone. A hello is greeted with a snarl.

Thirty minutes before trying to match Vander Meer's record, Ryan joked with reporters in the clubhouse. "I like to talk to people before a game," he once reported. "It keeps my mind off the game."

The hitters wish there was something to take their minds off Ryan's fastball.

By striking out 13 Orioles and 17 Tigers (most ever in a no-hitter), Ryan equaled the American League record for strikeouts in two consecutive nine-inning games held by Sudden Sam McDowell.

With 41 strikeouts in three games, Nolan broke by one the record he shared with Sudden Sam.

His sudden fame after so many years of struggling for control has left Ryan, like Sandy Koufax, unaffected. When the Angels arrived at a remote freight hangar at L.A. International Airport after his second no-hitter, about 20 fans were waiting.

A fence prevented the fans from getting close to the team bus. The fence didn't prevent Ryan from walking 50 yards out of his way, signing autographs and rapping until the team was ready to leave.

He was the same Ryan after losing the bid for a double no-no against the Orioles as after beating the Tigers. He was more anxious to talk about his appreciation for the crowd than the fates that cheated him of a record third no-hitter.

"I enjoyed the crowd," he said as calmly as a man reporting home from a day selling shoes. "They were appreciative. That means a lot to someone performing.

"To me, that's the greatest reward in baseball, fans appreciating your effort."

RYAN BREAKS SANDY'S WHIFF RECORD

by DICK MILLER

October 13, 1973

ANAHEIM—Harry Dalton had an interesting idea after the Angels' Nolan Ryan broke Sandy Koufax's single-season strikeout record against Minnesota September 27 at Anaheim Stadium.

"They ought to resurrect Cy Young," suggested the general manager, "and give him the Nolan Ryan Award."

Ryan's 16 strikeouts give him a season total of 383.

It is one of life's little ironies that if an umpire hadn't taken an out away from an Oakland batter nearly a month ago, Ryan would have to pitch again on the last day of the season, needing another strikeout to break the record.

The scene: Ryan had a 3-and-2 count on Oakland's Deron Johnson in the ninth inning of a September 3 game at Anaheim Stadium. On the next pitch, Johnson apparently popped out to second baseman Sandy Alomar.

Wait a second! Third base umpire Art Frantz yelled he called time before the pitch. A ball had been thrown out of the Angel bullpen.

Amidst boos from the crowd, Ryan was ordered to pitch again to the A's designated hitter. Johnson struck out on the next pitch. And without that strikeout, Ryan and Koufax would be tied.

The scoreboard in Anaheim tells the story as Ryan strikes out his 383rd batter of the 1973 season, breaking Sandy Koufax's single-season strikeout record.

RYAN'S RECORDS ADDING TO NEWSPRINT SHORTAGE

by DICK MILLER   **OCTOBER 27, 1973**

ANAHEIM—In an era when the world is running out of gasoline, beef is in short supply and there isn't enough electricity, Nolan Ryan is an unlikely contributor to the energy crisis.

The Ryan Express is adding to the paper shortage.

If you don't believe it, check with the publishers who have to rewrite the baseball records after the Angel pitcher's performance during the '73 season.

Ryan broke Sandy Koufax's modern season strikeout record with his final pitch of the season. An inside fastball made Rich Reese of Minnesota his 383rd victim of the season.

He threw two no-hitters—and with any luck would have doubled that figure. Winning his last seven decisions in succession with complete games, Ryan finished the season with 21 victories for a team that was last in the American League in hitting, runs batted in and home runs.

The comparisons with Koufax are inevitable. At the age of 26, the Dodger Hall of Famer had 68 victories. Ryan has 69. Koufax set a record by striking out 10 or more batters 21 times in a single season. Ryan did it 23 times last season.

Koufax set the modern record (since 1900) with 699 strikeouts in consecutive seasons. Ryan had 712 in 1972-73.

He'll try to do better next season.

"I really feel I can do better," he admitted. "I did about as well as I can the last month, but not seasonwise. I think I can have a better winning percentage.

"My control needs improving," continued Ryan. "I think I can cut down on the walks and throw fewer pitches and not have so much strain." In breaking Koufax's record, Ryan threw 205 pitches in 11 innings. "I walked 162 this season and I've led the league in walks the last two years.

"I think I can get it down to about 100 because I've got better rhythm than I used to have. That's 60 people I'd be keeping off base."

The designated-hitter rule played a part in Ryan's strikeout record. He might have struck out 400 if he was facing pitchers instead of designated hitters. On the other hand, the rule kept him in games longer. He worked 326 innings while completing 26 of 39 starts.

While leading the major leagues with 329 strikeouts in 1972, Ryan fanned the pitcher 42 times. Although he worked more innings in '73 (326 to 284), he struck out designated hitters only 30 times.

> **"I really feel I can do better," he admitted. "I did about as well as I can the last month, but not seasonwise. I think I can have a better winning percentage."**

Ryan's Major Accomplishments in 1973

- Major league record (since 1900), strikeouts, season: 383 (old mark, Koufax, 382 in 1965)
- Major league record, strikeouts, consecutive seasons: 712 (old modern mark 699 by Koufax in 1965-66)
- Major league record, 10-or-more strikeouts in a game: 23 times (old mark 21, by Koufax in 1965)
- Major league record, strikeouts, three consecutive games, tie: 41 in 27 innings (is also held by Koufax—28 innings—in 1959 and Luis Tiant—28 innings—in 1968)
- American League record, strikeouts, two consecutive games (18 innings), tie: 30 (also held by McDowell in 1968)
- Club record, wins, season, righthander: 21 (old mark, Chance, 20 in 1964)
- Club record, complete games, season: 26 (old mark, Ryan, 20 in 1972)
- Club record, consecutive complete games: 7 (old mark 6, by Ryan in 1972)
- Club record, consecutive complete-game victories: 7 (old mark 5, by Ryan in 1972)
- Club record, innings, season: 326 (old mark 284, by Ryan in 1972)
- Club record, strikeouts, game, tie: 17 (also held by Ryan, 17 vs. Minnesota September 20, 1972)
- Averaged 10.57 strikeouts per nine innings pitched
- Pitched two no-hit victories (only Virgil Trucks, Allie Reynolds and John Vander Meer had done so in one season): May 15, 3-0 at Kansas City, 12 strikeouts; July 15, 6-0 at Detroit, 17 strikeouts
- Had two nine-inning one-hitters: July 19 vs. Baltimore (lost on 3-hitter in 10⅓ innings, 3-1); August 29 vs. New York, won 5-0
- Only third man in history to strike out 300 in back-to-back seasons
- Combined with Bill Singer (241) for 624 strikeouts, major league record for one season by two men on same staff (old mark—592 by Don Drysdale, 210, and Koufax, 382, in 1965)
- Struck out designated hitters 30 times (struck out pitchers 42 times in 1972)
- Struck out the side 22 times (11 times in 1972)
- Struck out Rod Carew, 1972 and 1973 batting champion, nine times in 1973 to equal individual high, and 14 times in two years, more than any other batter vs. Ryan

FEW INCHES DEPRIVED RYAN OF THE BIG PRIZE

by DICK MILLER   **NOVEMBER 24, 1973**

ANAHEIM—Nolan and Ruth Ryan were attending class at Alvin (Texas) Junior College when word was received that the Angels' pitcher had finished second to the Orioles' Jim Palmer in the American League Cy Young balloting.

Two no-hitters, 21 victories for the worst-hitting team in the American League and breaking Sandy Koufax's single-season strikeout record weren't enough to overcome Palmer's early showing.

Would four no-hitters have changed the voters' thinking?

It probably would have, especially if one of them had tied Johnny Vander Meer's record for consecutive no-hitters.

Ryan came within five feet of back-to-back no-hitters and within six inches of another no-hitter. Four in one season would have matched Koufax's entire career output.

"I don't know what a guy has to do to win the award," Angels general manager Harry Dalton said after the announcement. "What really upsets me is four guys didn't even put him on the ballot at all.

"But," he added, "I can't really quarrel with the selection of Palmer. He's an excellent choice. What really killed Nolan was the second-place votes and the early impression Palmer made."

Palmer collected 14 first-place votes to Ryan's nine and six second places to three for the Angels' righthander.

The difference was probably a matter of luck.

Ryan threw a no-hitter at Kansas City May 15. Four days later at Anaheim, he had another no-hitter going into the eighth inning. Mark Belanger then looped a short fly to center field that Ken Berry, who was playing far too deep for the light-hitting shortstop, missed catching by one step.

Ryan went on to lose a three-hitter in eleven innings.

A one-hitter against the Yankees August 29 was even more heartbreaking. In the first inning, Thurman Munson was hit on the fists by a fastball.

The ball popped toward the grass behind second base, where both second baseman Sandy Alomar and shortstop Rudy Meoli were in position to catch it. Both called for it at the same time and both backed off at the same time, allowing it to fall free.

It went as the only hit of the game.

Not only is baseball a game of inches, but it turns out awards also are a matter of inches. If Ryan had been successful in the two near-misses, there's no way The Express could have missed being the second Cy Young winner in the Angels' history.

Ryan, who won his last seven starts with complete-game victories, figured Palmer was the man he had to beat.

"At first I thought it would be Catfish Hunter," said Ryan, "but the more I thought about it, I figured it would be Palmer. He had more impressive statistics."

The Ryans have been taking two classes at Alvin Jaycee: income tax preparation and beef cattle raising.

He should have no beef about his salary next season. Despite losing the Cy Young balloting, he should become the first $100,000 pitcher in the Angels' history.

Ryan has some terrible news for his A.L. rivals. He believes he will be a better pitcher next season, although some baseball people think the 326 innings he worked will take something out of his arm.

"I don't think so," said Ryan. "I don't think it took anything out of myself physically. Next year I think my control (he walked 162 batters) will be better and I'll hold runners on base better."

His success isn't likely to go to his handsome head. Ruth usually answers all phone calls to their 8½-acre ranch. On the day of the balloting, she reported, "He's out working in the back pasture with the dogs. He'll call you back when he gets home at dark."

FIREBALLER RYAN UNANIMOUS PICK FOR HELMS AWARD

by DICK MILLER   **January 12, 1974**

ANAHEIM—Santa Claus must have been tipped off about the energy crisis years ago because he ordered the all-new nine-reindeer sled with all the options. Anyhow, Santa was an early visitor at the Nolan Ryan residence in Alvin, Texas.

Santa, who refused to come into the house until the Ryans turned off a record of Gene Autry singing "Rudolph, the Red-Nosed Reindeer," left presents for Ryan, wife Ruth, and the little Choo Choo, two-year-old Reid. They were opened on Christmas Eve.

On the package was marked, "Do Not Open Until Christmas."

It was one of the nicest presents of all. The kindly elves at the United Savings Helms Hall of Fame sent the Angels' 21-game winner a scroll proclaiming him as Southern California's Athlete of the Year for 1973.

He may have finished second in the Cy Young Award voting, but Ryan beat out a tougher field to win the Southern California honor. He was the unanimous choice, beating such super stars as Bill Walton of UCLA and John Hadl of the Rams.

"We think it is a great honor," said spokesman Buddy Dyer, "because there are more great athletes in Southern California than any section of the country. And for Ryan to be elected unanimously this year is really something."

Ryan was in the back pasture, building a shed for his bull, when a call was placed to his ranch to tell him about the honor. In the midst of planning for the holidays, Ruth Ryan took time out from wrapping presents to tell what the award meant.

"We're really excited about it," said Ryan's winter manager.

The only present missing under the Ryans' Christmas tree was a pennant.

If he hadn't been traded by the Mets to the Angels with three other players for Jim Fregosi, Ryan probably would have changed the course of last year's World Series.

Ruth isn't sure whether she and her man would have liked that. Anaheim's population of 168,000 is closer to Alvin's 15,000 than the 10 million who inhabit New York.

"It was very exciting being in New York," recalled Mrs. Ryan. "It was exciting having people recognize you wherever you went. But Nolan prefers Anaheim. He likes his privacy. If he had his choice, he would play in Anaheim. Out here we can go shopping and no one bothers him."

He may not have much time left as the Unknown Pitcher. If he throws a couple more no-hitters and strikes out 400 batters next season, Ryan will replace Mickey Mouse, Walter Knott and Walt Disney as the best-known men in Orange County.

AP/Wide World Photos

Ryan pitches to his son Reid at the Ryans' home in Anaheim.

4

HEATING UP

NOLAN RYAN

The legend of the Ryan Express continued to grow after Ryan's second no-hitter. On August 12, 1974, he fanned 19 Boston batters, tying the then-major-league record for strikeouts in a nine-inning game. Later that season he set a new speed record when his fastball was officially clocked at 100.8 miles per hour, and also tied yet another major-league record when he pitched his third no-hitter. On June 1, 1975, he became the only pitcher other than Sandy Koufax to have more than three no-hitters when he accomplished the feat for the fourth time. Everything was going Ryan's way until his season ended prematurely in September due to bone chips in his elbow. Ryan underwent surgery and hoped to return better than ever.

Reid Ryan, 2, checks out his father's pitching arm at their home in Anaheim.

AP/Wide World Photos

RYAN REDDENS AT NEW WORK SCHEDULE

by DICK MILLER   **AUGUST 3, 1974**

ANAHEIM—Happiness is a winning ball club. Unless the manager is Dick Williams. The controversial new skipper of the Angels managed the anarchy- and anger-ridden Oakland club into two world championships.

After only three weeks on the job in Anaheim, Williams found his judgement being challenged from a surprising quarter. Nolan Ryan flirted with another no-hitter at Cleveland July 15 and afterward admitted his disappoinment that Williams has gone to a five-man pitching rotation.

He prefers to work every fourth day come rainouts, doubleheaders and days off.

"It's going to be tough for me to win," said Ryan, choosing his words carefully. "Tonight is a good example (he walked seven). I'm a completely different pitcher.

"I've lost my rhythm. A good example is the way I pitched tonight. It was the same way with the Mets."

The switch, according to pitching coach Tom Morgan, was made to save wear and tear on Ryan's arm and the young pitching staff.

"Some way to save your arm," said Ryan. "Throw 200 pitches a game. When Whitey (interim manager between Bobby Winkles and Williams) took over, he said I would be pitching every fifth day."

"I'm not going to pitch him every fourth day and mess up other pitchers," said Williams, assuming a posture that would never be mistaken for a Henry Kissinger.

"My job," said Williams, "is to build up a good starting mound staff and organization. I'm going to do it. We have a fellow named Lange...a fellow named Hasler...a guy named Figueroa...five guys in the bullpen...a guy named Chalk...someone named Robinson.

"We're all in this together."

19 WHIFFS... SOME DAY RYAN MAY STRIKE OUT 27

by DICK MILLER   **AUGUST 31, 1974**

ANAHEIM—Nolan Ryan doesn't believe it is humanly possible for any major league pitcher to strike out every batter (27) in a major league game. But he may come close some day.

All it will take is: (a) a free-swinging team like Boston, Detroit or Kansas City; (b) a 100 mph

fastball and (c) a more sympathetic umpire like the retired Ed Runge, whose heart was a mile wide and who had a strike zone to match.

Reflecting back on August 12, when he fanned 19 Boston batters to equal the record for a nine-inning game shared by the Mets' Tom Seaver and the Phils' Steve Carlton, then with the Cardinals, Ryan thought he could have recorded two or three more strikeouts.

This, of course, wouldn't leave much work for Ryan's infielders and outfielders, who had to record only eight outs.

Only three of the 19 strikeouts were called by plate umpire Marty Springstead, who called a remarkably consistent game. While not questioning the veteran arbiter's judgment, Ryan thought more Boston batters could have been called out.

"He didn't miss any," said Ryan, "but he didn't give us any. If a pitcher is going to strike out 20 or more, he's going to have to have more called strikes."

In the history of professional baseball, only one pitcher has struck out all 27 batters in a game. Surely you remember that Ron Necciai, the Bristol Bullet, struck out every Welch batter one summer day in 1952 in the Appalachian League.

The Bullet must have spent itself that day. Summoned to Pittsburgh, Necciai won exactly one game in his two years in the majors.

Ryan received more standing ovations from the Anaheim Stadium crowd than a Metropolitan Opera diva. Ironically, Ryan was the victim of Carlton's 19-strikeout performance against the Mets and was on the Mets bench when Seaver turned in his record performance at San Diego.

It was a 3-and-2 fastball to pinch-hitter Bernie Carbo in the ninth inning—a called strike by Springstead—that broke Bob Feller's 35-year-old American League strikeout record and tied Seaver and Carlton.

Ryan got two strikes on the next batter, Rick Burleson, but the shortstop lined to right field to end the game.

Ryan struck out every Red Sox batter except Burleson and fanned at least one batter in every inning. He struck out the side in the second, fourth and eighth innings. Two strikeouts were recorded in each of the first, sixth, seventh and ninth innings, with a single strikeout in the third and fifth innings.

In his previous start five days earlier, Ryan had taken a no-hitter into the ninth inning at Chicago only to lose a heartbreaker.

Ryan, who still has as much country boy in him as Tennessee Ernie Ford and Jim Nabors, honestly wasn't surprised by the 19 strikeouts.

"I felt one day I would have a chance to do this if everything went right," he said. "At the start of

the game, I didn't think I had the same rhythm as at Chicago. It got better as I went along."

No one ever will know how hard Ryan was throwing, but manager Dick Williams laughed and said, "His changeup was faster than most guys' fastballs."

The Angel front office, in cooperation with North American-Rockwell Co., is planning a test to measure Ryan's fastball soon.

Ryan was asked to compare the 19 strikeouts to last year's no-hitters against Kansas City and Detroit.

"The no-hitters are a greater achievement. There's no margin for error in a no-hitter," he said.

He still rates breaking Sandy Koufax's single-season strikeout record (with 383) last season over the no-hitters.

"The no-hitters gained more notoriety," he noted, "but the strikeout record meant more. It was over the long haul."

Ryan said he wasn't aware he was getting close to the record until he glanced at the scoreboard in the seventh or eighth inning.

An error by shortstop Bobby Valentine enabled Ryan to break Feller's American League record and tie the all-time mark. There was one out in the ninth inning with runners on first and second base when Boston's Doug Griffin hit an easy double-play grounder to Valentine.

He booted it. To some press box observers, it looked like it was a deliberate error to keep Ryan's record chances alive. The Express made the next batter, Carbo, his record victim.

If Valentine made the error on purpose, it was a courageous risk, one that could have made him a legendary goat if Ryan had not been able to blaze his way out of the jam.

"I wouldn't do that," said Valentine emphatically. "I play to win."

Ryan had trouble with only two batters, leadoff man Juan Beniquez and second baseman Doug Griffin, in winning his 15th game, 4-2. Beniquez had three hits, including a triple. Facing Ryan for the first time since one of his fastballs hit him in the head April 30, Griffin had two singles and was safe on the ninth-inning error.

Where does he go from here? The Express in less than two seasons has thrown a pair of no-hitters, broken Koufax's single-season strikeout record, tied the all-time single game record and won 21 games for a team that would be rejected by the Salvation Army.

Ryan shows off a ball from his 19-strikeout game against the Boston Red Sox.

Some baseball people, including Ryan, think he will be traded next winter. The super scouts, general managers and personnel directors appear to outnumber the fans at Anaheim Stadium on the nights when the Ryan Express is due to barrel down the track.

He prefers to stay in Anaheim despite the club's clouded future.

"I wouldn't want to be traded," he said recently. "Houston or Dallas would be the only places I'd want to go. I enjoy living in Anaheim. It's more to my lifestyle.

"I believe they have to trade one front-line pitcher. It will be either Willie (the injured Bill Singer) or me."

He admits he is trying for records in the final days of the longest season. "When you are out of everything like we are, you have to try to salvage something," he said.

RYAN NEW SPEED KING, CLOCKED AT 100.8 MPH

by DICK MILLER   **SEPTEMBER 21, 1974**

ANAHEIM—Nolan Ryan has broken Bob Feller's longtime record but left unanswered a question baseball fans have been asking since the days of Walter Johnson:

How fast is it humanly possible to throw a baseball? Feller's unofficial record of 98.6 has been recognized since 1946.

Ryan broke the speed record twice against the White Sox, clocking 98.8 and 100.8 miles per hour at Anaheim Stadium September 7. The tests were certified by a team of four Rockwell International scientists who operated an infra-red radar device from the press box.

But it turned out that while he may have broken Feller's 28-year-old record, Ryan missed by one-tenth of a mile per hour breaking his own unreported record set 18 days earlier.

The same team of Rockwell International scientists had clocked Ryan at 100.9 mph in the second inning of a game against Detroit on August 20.

George Lederer, the public relations director of the Angels who set up the tests, said he preferred to have the slower 100.8 figure recognized. "Some refinements were made after the original tests," said Lederer.

In either case, it now appears Ryan is capable of throwing at least five miles per hour faster. He did not have his good stuff during the official test, Ryan and press box observers agreeing he had one of the poorest fastballs of the season.

Ryan also didn't have his good velocity early in the August 20 test, which saw him pick up speed in the fourth inning and go on to break Feller's American League record for strikeouts in a single game with 19.

Although Ryan's speeds were not announced until after

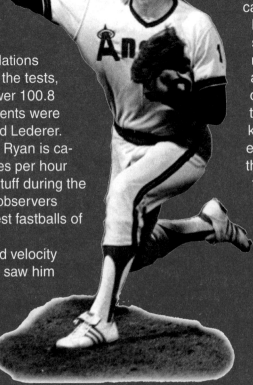

AP/Wide World Photos

the final out, the Express admitted the pressure of the situation got to him. He had not thrown well since striking out 19 Red Sox batters on August 28 and spent most of the two hours before the game taping an interview for CBS Sports Spectacular.

"I didn't like it," he admitted. "It takes too much away from your concentration. Winning the game is still the most important thing. I don't know if they picked up every pitch. A lot of balls outside the strike zone have more velocity."

The radar not only was unable to pick up balls outside of the strike zone but what would have been over the outside corner for right-handed hitters.

White Sox players agreed Ryan didn't have his good stuff during the test. The record-breaking pitch of 98.8 mph was clocked with Bee Bee Richard at bat in the ninth inning.

Tom Egan was behind the plate for the record-setter. "I've caught him when he threw harder than he did tonight," said Egan. "He didn't have his real stuff. All that activity took away from his concentration. I don't know why there is all that fuss anyhow. Everybody knows he's the fastest that ever lived. The only important thing is for him to win 20 and the experiment nearly ruined that."

A contest to guess Ryan's speed and number of pitches—he threw 159—drew national interest. The 6,200 entries came from 38 states, including 282 communities in California alone. A total of 55 entries guessed his speed exactly with the winner missing the correct total by one pitch.

RYAN ROARS INTO FELLER'S CLASS WITH 3RD GEM

by DICK MILLER   **OCTOBER 12, 1974**

In these trying inflationary times prices continue to spiral on all commodities.

On September 28, the price on Nolan Ryan went so far out of sight not even J. Paul Getty and Ari Onassis—or the Los Angeles Dodgers—apparently will be able to afford the Angels' righthander this winter.

Ryan did his thing against the Twins, throwing the third no-hitter of his career in beating the Twins 4-0 with 15 strikeouts. Only Sandy Koufax, with four, has thrown more no-hitters in a career than the 27-year-old righthander.

The Express walked eight in tying Bob Feller's American League record for no-hitters and likely took himself out of the trade market. How can any club now, even the talent-rich Dodgers, come up with enough players to make the Angels a contender and pry Ryan away from Harry Dalton?

For weeks there had been reports that fabulous packages were being readied for a man who has thrown three no-hitters in the span of two years, struck out 19 batters in a game three times this season, and pitched four one-hitters.

Ryan, who prefers to stay with the Angels if he isn't traded to the Astros, doubts now he will be traded this winter. "I can't see any club weakening itself that much by trading for a pitcher," he said the day after making baseball history again.

No-hitters are almost becoming routine with Ryan. He has learned to take his telephone off the hook. He doesn't become excited after performing one of the rarest feats in sports. "I try to take it in stride," he said simply.

The 10,872 fans at Anaheim Stadium didn't. After the final out, Ryan nonchalantly walked off the mound as the crowd let out a roar. Ryan was mobbed by his teammates from the bench, who met him at the foul line, and the Angels' bullpen raced in from the outfield to join the celebration.

Ryan went into the dugout, but as the thunderous applause continued from the seats, he returned to the field, tipped his hat and posed for photographers.

"I felt like I might have a good game," he admitted later. "I warmed up well and the first pitch had good velocity." His first seven pitches were strikes and he fanned the side in the first and second innings.

> "I felt like I might have a good game," he admitted later. "I warmed up well and the first pitch had good velocity."

He was asked to compare his performance with last year's no-hitters at Kansas City and Detroit. "I had better stuff than in the first one and about the equivalent with the one in Detroit. But my control wasn't as sharp."

The victory was Ryan's 22nd, tying Clyde Wright's club record. The 15 strikeouts gave him a total of 367 for the season and a chance to equal his own all-time record of 383 by working the final game of the season.

"I'd like a couple of days to see how my arm responds before deciding," he said.

Outside of Ryan, Koufax, and Feller, only two other pitchers have thrown three no-hitters: Larry Corcoran of the Chicago Cubs and Cincinnati's Jim Maloney.

"It was a struggle," admitted Ryan. "Anytime you are as wild as I was it's a struggle." Ryan walked seven in the first five innings to make him the first major league pitcher to walk more than 200 in a season since Bob Feller did it in 1938.

AP/Wide World Photos

Teammates congratulate Ryan after the third no-hitter of his career.

Tom Egan, who was catching when Ryan broke Feller's speed record, turned in an excellent game behind the plate.

Until the no-hitter, there was widespread speculation Ryan would be traded this winter. According to which newspaper you were reading, this is where the Express was headed:

The Angels will trade Nolan Ryan to Houston this winter for first baseman Lee May, third baseman Doug Rader and pitcher Don Wilson.

Or, San Francisco will win the bidding war for pitcher Ryan's services with an offer of outfielder Bobby Bonds and infielder-outfielder Dave Kingman.

Or, sometime during the winter meetings, the White Sox will win out with an offer of third baseman Bill Melton, outfielder Ken Henderson plus either catcher Ed Herrmann or relief pitcher Rich Gossage.

Blessed with probably more excess tradeable talent than any club in baseball, the Dodgers supposedly have a list of expendables headed by outfielder Bill Buckner. They'll be available when the winter trading season begins at 12:01 a.m. PDT five days after the conclusion of the World Series.

Or, none of the above.

What is fact and what is fiction?

It is fact that the Angels desperately need a right-handed power hitter to replace the departed Frank Robinson and Bob Oliver. The Angel farm system is beginning to produce players at an accelerated pace, but none of the right-handed hitters is expected to be ready by next spring.

And it is a fact that Ryan is the lone player

whose value is so high both at the box office and on the field that he could give the Angels instant respectability by bringing three or four players in trade.

Playing with a contender, Ryan might have won 30 games this season. At 27, the righthander presumably has his best years ahead of him.

Can Harry Dalton afford to trade his lone big name and drawing card, now that Frank Robinson is at Cleveland? With only two years to go on his long-term contract and no progress in the standings, the general manager may be forced to make a bold move.

Ryan isn't anxious to leave Orange County, although he confided recently, "I'd buy my own bus ticket to get to Houston."

From unimpeachable sources, it has been learned the Astros intend to break up their club this winter in their disappointment over not becoming a contender. The scouting report on May, 31, is that he is still capable of playing first base for another year and then could be utilized as a designated hitter.

Dalton has said he doubts he will trade Ryan. But if the Angels are offered two quality regular players, a pitcher of stature and a pitching prospect, he may find the temptation irresistible.

The general manager was unavailable for comment when the subject of a Ryan trade came up. He was in San Francisco on a scouting mission. That was interesting, since Charlie Fox, the Giants' former manager and current super scout, spent two weeks bird-dogging the Angels in August.

Asked whom the Giants were interested in, Fox smiled and said, "They have only one player, Ryan."

Admitting he can feel his career slipping away with the downtrodden Angels, Ryan said, "The only place I would want to be traded to is Houston or Dallas. You reach a point of frustration. You'd like to be able to see on the horizon that you are on a pennant contender or a winner and that the winning involves you.

"I'd like to stay in Southern California. Anaheim is more my lifestyle, although I wouldn't mind going to the Dodgers. They would have to drag me to San Francisco."

September 28, 1974
California 4, Minnesota 0

MINNESOTA	ab	r	h	bi	CALIFORNIA	ab	r	h	bi
Brye cf	2	0	0	0	M. Nettles cf	4	1	2	3
Carew 2b	2	0	0	0	D. Doyle 2b	4	0	1	0
Braun 3b	3	0	0	0	Bochte 1b	3	0	0	1
Darwin rf	4	0	0	0	Lahoud dh	4	0	1	0
Oliva dh	3	0	0	0	Stanton rf	4	0	1	0
Hisle lf	3	0	0	0	Chalk 3b	2	1	0	0
Bourque 1b	3	0	0	0	Balaz lf	2	1	1	0
Killebrew ph	0	0	0	0	Meoli ss	2	1	1	0
Terrell pr	0	0	0	0	Egan c	2	0	0	0
Gomez ss	2	0	0	0					
Soderholm ss	2	0	0	0					
Borgmann c	3	0	0	0					
TOTALS	27	0	0	0		27	4	7	4

Minnesota	0 0 0	0 0 0	0 0 0—0
California	0 0 2	2 0 0	0 0 x—4

E—Braun. LOB—Minnesota 8, California 4. 2B—Meoli, Balaz. SB—M. Nettles. S—Egan. SF—Bochte.

MINNESOTA	IP	H	R	ER	BB	SO
Decker (L 16-14)	2⅔	4	2	1	0	1
Butler	5⅓	3	2	2	3	8
CALIFORNIA						
Ryan (W 22-16)	9	0	0	0	8	15

WIFE PITCHING IN TO HELP RYAN CATCH WHIFF LEADERS

by DICK MILLER   **FEBRUARY 22, 1975**

ANAHEIM—In these traumatic times, it is a pleasure to present the heartwarming saga of Nolan and Ruth Ryan.

Behind every successful man, the cliché goes, stands a woman. Some marital experts are quick to add that the woman is shoving. In the case of Nolan Ryan, super pitcher, and Ruth Ryan, super wife, the woman was standing 60 feet, six inches in front of the man and holding a catcher's mitt.

In tuning up for spring training, Ryan has been working out four or five times a week in the backyard of his home in Alvin, Texas.

"I've been working out with a high school catcher," reported Ryan. "When he doesn't show up, I play with Ruth. She's throwing harder than I am."

Some American League hitters swing at the sound of Ryan's fastball, claiming it shows up only on radar. In his last start of the 1974 season, Ryan threw a no-hitter against Minnesota, and thus will be going for back-to-back no-hitters in the Angels' season opener April 5 against Kansas City.

If Ruthie only had a little more power and got rid of the ball a little faster, Harry Dalton might be tempted to sign the husband-and-wife team as an entry, sort of like Koufax and Drysdale. "I throw the ball as hard as she can catch it," The Express reported.

"She handles it better than some catchers I've had."

Ryan's salary will advance him to the superstar class this season. The Express worked for $100,000 in 1974, responding with 22 wins, his annual no-hitter and 367 strikeouts. He is expected to work for around $150,000 this season.

Ryan thinks he will be even better in '75 with added maturity and confidence. A study of the great pitchers of baseball history agrees with The Ex-

press' contention, "I'm looking forward to my best season ever. I have more confidence in myself."

Ryan celebrated his 28th birthday January 31. He will be happy to know that he is entering his prime of life as a power pitcher.

A statistical study of the all-time top 15 strikeout pitchers shows that nine of them attained their peak after age 27, including Hall of Fame members Sandy Koufax, Early Wynn, Rube Waddell, Cy Young, Warren Spahn and Tim Keefe.

Of the top 15 all-time strikeout leaders, nine already are in the Hall of Fame. Robin Roberts, Bob Gibson, Don Drysdale and Jim Bunning all have good chances of winding up in Cooperstown with Mickey Lolich and Sudden Sam McDowell having lesser chances.

Ryan, who has rewritten most of the strikeout records in his three seasons with the Angels, already ranks No. 1 with his average of 9.74 strikeouts per nine innings. Next are McDowell (8.87), Lolich (7.32) and Gibson (7.29).

He doesn't intend to change his pitching style to save wear on his arm. "I think I'll be a power pitcher the rest of my career," he said.

"I'd like to pitch five more years, but that could change. When you reach a certain age, it's frustrating not to be on a pennant contender. You start looking for other things.

"It has been frustrating the last three years. You can't enjoy the season, you are constantly under pressure. I feel like I have to pitch a shutout every night or lose. I can't afford to make a mistake, to give up a hit."

At his current pace of 196 strikeouts through eight major league seasons, Ryan could rank seventh on the all-time list after only five more seasons. If he maintains his average of 360 strikeouts since arriving in Anaheim, Ryan would crash the top 15 two weeks into the 1977 season.

Most power pitches are just beginning to reach their prime at 28.

Koufax showed the best record of the post-27 group with an average of 307 strikeouts for three years. Next are Lolich (225 for seven years), Gibson (215 for 11 years) and Waddell (208 for seven years).

There have been some notable exceptions, according to the statistical survey compiled by the Angels' George Lederer. McDowell, who ranks 10th all-time with 2,424 strikeouts, averaged 218 for nine seasons through age 27 and only 91 for the last five years. Feller, No. 6 all-time, has a 205 average for eight years through age 27 and dropped to an average of 94 for his last 10 years.

Service in World War II undoubtedly had something to do with the drop in Feller's strikeouts.

It was reported last season that Ryan expected to pitch only three more years. In that case, the story went, he would just as soon pitch every third day and risk injury to his right arm.

"I still say if it makes a difference in a pennant race, I would pitch every third day," said Ryan. "Under the present circumstances, I'd prefer to work in the regular four-man rotation.

"The way things look now, Texas could win it. I don't think Oakland will be near the threat they have been without Catfish Hunter. The dynasty is about to crumble. But you don't know what Charlie Finley is going to do.

"If he trades one of his regulars for a pitcher, my choice would be Reggie Jackson. He would tear up the National League where he would see more fastballs."

Barring an injury, Ryan should continue throwing no-hitters, striking out batters by the gross and, most important of all, winning. His total of 91 wins, through age 27, is ahead of such greats at a comparable age as Spahn (44), Wynn (64), Bunning (59), Gibson (52), Lolich (55) and Waddell (74).

Koufax had only two more wins, 93, at the same age.

Ruth Ryan helped her husband gear up for spring training in 1975.

AP/Wide World Photos

MODEST RYAN STANDS TALL WITH TEAMMATES

by DICK MILLER　　　**MARCH 22, 1975**

HOLTVILLE—Some Angel players who hadn't received a fan letter in months were surprised to find an envelope in their boxes when they reported for work at Anaheim Stadium last September 29.

Inside each envelope was a $100 check signed by Nolan Ryan.

Quietly and without fanfare, The Express was saying thanks to his teammates who had played a part in his third no-hitter the night before, a 4-0 victory over Minnesota.

Six months later, the modest superstar of the Angels still is reluctant to talk about his act of generosity. In a day when sports stars jump contracts and make outrageous salary demands, Ryan remains a small-town boy from Alvin, Texas.

A two-year contract that calls for him to receive $125,000 this season hasn't changed one of the hardest throwers in baseball history. Ryan knows what it is like to be broke.

He almost quit baseball three springs ago when his money was giving out and his wife was expecting their first child. If the players' strike had lasted another two weeks, Ruth Ryan believes her husband would have quit baseball.

The details behind Ryan's no-hitter in his final start of the 1974 season have never been told before. The day after this feat, general manager Harry Dalton tore up Nolan's contract and gave him a $2,000 raise. Catcher Tom Egan was given a new contract, too, calling for a $500 raise.

That afternoon, Ryan sat down and wrote out the checks, giving away nearly half of his bonus.

The Nolan Ryan Story is the kind Hollywood used to make movies about before the disaster cycle. It is the story of a pitcher who is as American as apple pie.

Ryan is the Angels' superstar in the clubhouse as well as on the mound. He is the club's player representative, selected by his teammates.

"He's always had to work hard," said Ruth. "Nolan started working at 8," recalled his high school sweetheart. "He bought his first car at 14 with his own money. He used to get up at 2 o'clock in the morning to roll papers and deliver the *Houston Post*. He'd get back home at 4 or 5 in the morning and go back to bed before going to school.

"One of the reasons he is the way he is," she added, "is that he is the youngest of six kids."

The man who has thrown three no-hitters the last two seasons, broke Sandy Koufax's single-season strikeout mark and became the first pitcher in baseball history to strike out 300 batters in three consecutive seasons nearly quit before pitching a game for the Angels in the regular season.

Along with three other players, Ryan had been acquired from the Mets for Jim Fregosi, a six-time All-Star selection and owner Gene Autry's choice to manage the Angels some day.

Ryan was awful the spring of 1972. He averaged two walks an inning. He hit so many batters it ignited a brawl with the Giants.

Ryan was ready to quit baseball when the players went on strike.

"He was wild that first spring," Ruth recalled. "He had to drive back and forth between Anaheim and Palm Springs (about 250 miles round trip) every day because we couldn't afford to rent a house in Palm Springs. We already had one in Anaheim.

"I was feeling sorry for myself and he said, 'Why don't we go home?' At that point, he was pretty close to quitting. We had a new baby and he was worrying about me and we didn't know anybody. It was frustrating.

"Nolan started worrying about what we were going to do. There was a lot of pressure on top of his worrying about us.

"I felt he still needed that chance without military obligations that had interrupted his career with the Mets. But if that strike had lasted any longer, we would have gone home. Nobody had any money, and if rent had been up, we would have gone home."

The decision to stay paid off. The Ryans are building a new home today. They have 50 head of cattle. They own eight acres in Alvin and 200 near Gonzales, Texas. They have two bulls, one of which is named Egan, after his catcher in the last no-hitter.

He is more than a player to his teammates, although he turned 28 only in January.

"He is an inspiration," said pitcher Frank Tanana. "You sit there watching how the man works and you know how hard you have to work. He's a superstar, but you never see him jaking."

"That's the way he always has been," said his wife. "He's been really great. He doesn't let that bother him. There are a lot of demands on his time, but he's polite and honest. We believe in first things first. We do things together.

"We won't let anything take him away from home for more than a week. He tries to leave everything at the ball park. He was like that even with the Mets. It was hard seeing Nolan getting nowhere there. It was frustrating because he had a good arm."

More than 1,000 strikeouts later, it is different. Ryan has won 62 games in three years for a team that is out of contention by July each year. There were four rookies in the lineup last September when he recorded his annual no-hitter: Morris Nettles, Bruce Bochte, Dave Chalk and John Balaz.

Also receiving checks from Ryan were Denny Doyle, Joe Lahoud, Lee Stanton, Rudy Meoli and Egan. Meoli had been the shortstop in all of Ryan's no-hitters.

NIPPON SLUGGER, RYAN MAY CLASH IN TV DUEL

by DICK MILLER   **JUNE 7, 1975**

ANAHEIM—Here's the pitch Nolan Ryan is making to Sadaharu Oh: If the Babe Ruth of Japan will meet him in a post-season head-to-head confrontation, Oh can make $20,000 for every home run in a contest for television.

At $20,000 per strikeout, the Angels' super star could collect $180,000 himself.

Even a single strikeout would be worth more than any other strikeout in baseball's history, according to Ryan's agent.

Ryan issued the challenge while his agents, Mattgo Enterprises of New York, were negotiating with network television officials. "It's an outgrowth of this spring when he said he would like to bat against me," said Ryan.

"I'd like to pitch against him. It would be a challenge. It would either be Anaheim Stadium or Dodger Stadium and possibly on TV."

This is the way the contest would work: An inning would consist of a strikeout or home run. Ground balls and fly balls would not count.

"We may have to change it around somewhat," said Matt Murola of Mattgo, who acknowledged that his client would have an advantage under the proposed rules. Ryan's averaging slightly better than a strikeout an inning.

A home-run slugger hits one out of the park every 14 to 20 times at bat.

"It has to be something that is sustaining—it can't be over on one pitch," said Murola. "Baseball traditionally is a nine-inning game, so we came up with this formula.

"The figure ($20,000) exceeds anything any strikeout has ever been worth before. If a pitcher strikes out a guy to win the seventh game of the World Series, that's still only the difference between winning and losing share, about $10,000.

In a TV battle last season, Oh lost a homer-hitting contest to American home-run champion Henry Aaron.

Oh, the first baseman of the Tokyo Giants, had more than 600 career home runs.

RYAN'S PACE: FOUR NO-HITTERS IN TWO-YEAR SPAN

by DICK MILLER   **JUNE 14, 1975**

ANAHEIM—Reid Ryan's graduation party was a blast. On the day Master Ryan graduated from nursery school and was sprung for summer vacation, his father dropped by to order an extra round of ice cream to celebrate himself.

Reid (The Choo Choo) Ryan has the rest of the summer off. And Nolan (The Express) Ryan will be trying to become the first pitcher in baseball history to record five no-hitters.

The Angels' superstar tied Sandy Koufax's record with his fourth when he beat Baltimore, 1-0, at Anaheim Stadium on June 1.

Ryan has thrown a no-hitter once every 27.2 starts since getting the hang of it in his first no-no against Kansas City on May 15, 1973. The most overpowering figure in the game, Ryan has fired four no-hitters in 109 starts.

The man he ties in the record books was one of the first to hear about it and offer his congratulations.

"I heard about it on the radio," Sandy Koufax said with a laugh when contacted in Paso Robles, California. "I'm going to send him my congratulations in the morning. I'll give it to a guy on horseback and he'll take it to Western Union," said the Dodger Hall of Famer, now a country squire, living 12 miles from the nearest city.

Ruth Ryan and the Choo Choo were in the stands at Anaheim Stadium as eyewitnesses. So was Ryan's sister, Mrs. Marylou Williams of Chatsworth, California. The Ryans' Anaheim neighbors were out of town, including Mrs. Vel Smith.

Poor Mrs. Smith. She's the kind lady who has been handling Ryan's correspondence, about 1,500 pieces of mail a month, on a volunteer basis. It may quadruple before the end of the season.

"I just felt he was going to win, that's all—I had a strong feeling today," said Ruth.

The pitcher's first two no-hitters were on the road (at Kansas City and Detroit). She missed his annual no-hitter in 1974, having gone home to Texas to prepare their house while he made his final start of the season at the Big A.

Ruth had confidence in Nolan's young teammates, who had lost five consecutive games.

"I didn't have a feeling anyone would make a costly error," she said. "The play Jerry Remy made behind second base (in the seventh inning) was something else. I have a good feeling about these young players," she added.

"It goes for the wives, too. There's a good feeling among us. It's different than in past years."

Meanwhile, a fund-raising drive may be required for baseball's Hall of Fame at Cooperstown, New York. A new wing may be needed after the 1975 season to house exhibits on Ryan's no-hitters.

Only six pitchers in baseball history have thrown three or more no-hitters. Koufax and Ryan lead with four apiece. Those who pitched three are Cy Young, Larry Corcoran, Bob Feller and Jim Maloney.

Ryan certainly has defied the law of averages, which says that a no-hitter is thrown every 1,444 games in the majors.

There had been 195 nine-inning no-hitters pitched in 223,092 opportunities going into the 1975 season.

According to Ryan's Law, a no-hitter should be thrown every four months. The Express took his latest eye-popper calmly.

"I think I'd prefer to have an outstanding year," said the 28-year-old righthander. "You know, something like a 27-5 record. That way, people would know I was great all year rather than on just one day."

Ryan might have been calm about the historic occasion, but his teammates weren't.

"I feel like I pitched a no-hitter," said catcher Ellie Rodriguez. On the disabled list for 28 days with an injured ankle, Rodriguez had been put on the active roster only four hours before the game.

"It's better than going 4-for-4 and hitting a home run," said the catcher. "I just want to catch his fifth."

Rookie second baseman Remy had the only tough play.

"I've witnessed a no-hitter before," said Remy after taking a possible hit away from Tommy Davis in the seventh inning. The pinch-hitter chopped a high hopper over the mound and behind the second base.

Remy got rid of the ball quickly to nip Davis at first base, a decision that both Davis and Oriole manager Earl Weaver protested to umpire Hank Soar.

"I just hoped I could keep myself in position," said Remy. "I knew I had a chance to get him. I got rid of it as fast as I could."

"He called me out, so I was out," said Davis.

"I wouldn't want to see a guy lose a no-hitter because an umpire called a guy safe when he was out," said Weaver. "But in my heart, I thought he was safe."

Ryan fanned nine, walked four and threw 91 strikes among his 147 pitches.

Twelve of the pitches, including a final called third strike to Bobby Grich, were changeups.

No one was more thrilled than coach Jimmie Reese.

The beloved Reese, 69, and a former roommate of Babe Ruth, is Ryan's constant companion in spring training and when Reese makes a trip.

Their idea of a big night on the road is to order chocolate syrup over two scoops of vanilla ice cream.

Ryan hugs Ruth after his 4th no-hitter, June 1, 1975, at Anaheim Stadium.

"I may go home and have an extra scoop. In fact, I may go home and faint," said the man who is known affectionately as Donkey.

Starting as a bat boy with the Los Angeles Angels (Pacific Coast) in 1917, Reese has seen them all: the greats, the utility players, the drinkers, the women chasers, the high-class guys, the Ruths, Gehrigs and the Lazzeris and the anonymous.

"On top of everything," said Reese, "Nolan is such a nice guy."

Already anticipating the gates for Ryan's future starts, Angel president Red Patterson hadn't been so happy since that summer night in 1965 when Koufax pitched his fourth no-hitter, a perfect game against the Cubs at Dodger Stadium.

Patterson then was Dodger vice president in charge of publicity. Now the rookie president of the Angels smiled and said: "I'm just glad he is going to have a chance to set an all-time record of five no-hitters."

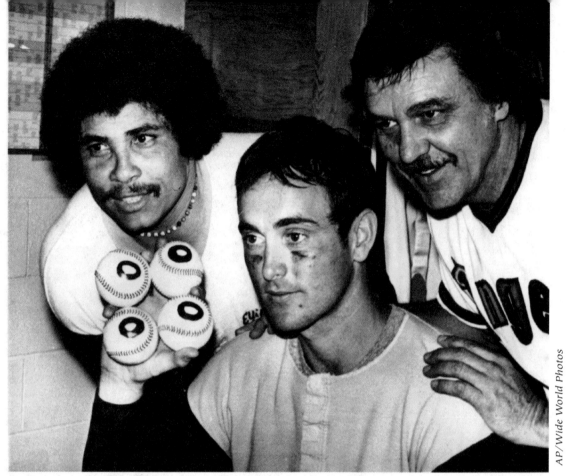

Ryan, joined by catcher Ellie Rodriguez (left) and manager Dick Williams, holds up four balls marked with the number 0 to symbolize his four no-hitters.

June 1, 1975
California 1, Baltimore 0

BALTIMORE	ab	r	h	bi		CALIFORNIA	ab	r	h	bi
Singleton rf	4	0	0	0		Remy 2b	3	0	1	0
Shopay cf	3	0	0	0		Rivers cf	4	1	1	0
Bumbry lf	4	0	0	0		Harper dh	4	0	1	0
Baylor dh	2	0	0	0		Chalk 3b	3	0	2	1
Davis dh	2	0	0	0		Llenas lf	3	0	1	0
Grich 2b	2	0	0	0		M. Nettles lf	0	0	0	0
May 1b	3	0	0	0		Stanton rf	2	0	1	0
Robinson 3b	3	0	0	0		Bochte 1b	3	0	1	0
Hendricks c	3	0	0	0		Rodriguez c	3	0	0	0
Belanger ss	2	0	0	0		Smith ss	2	0	1	0
TOTALS	28	0	0	0			27	1	9	1

Baltimore	0 0 0	0 0 0	0 0 0—0
California	0 0 1	0 0 0	0 0 0—1

E—Smith. DP—Baltimore 2. LOB—Baltimore 5, California 5. SB—Belanger. S—Stanton, Remy.

BALTIMORE	IP	H	R	ER	BB	SO
Grimsley (L 1-7)	3⅓	8	1	1	0	1
Garland	4⅔	1	0	0	1	1

CALIFORNIA						
Ryan (W 9-3)	9	0	0	0	4	9

ANGELS EAGER TO DEAL—EVEN RYAN MAY DEPART

by DICK MILLER   **AUGUST 30, 1975**

ANAHEIM—Will the Angels trade a pitcher who has thrown four no-hitters, won 20 games in successive seasons and broken Sandy Koufax's single-season strikeout record?

Probably.

The Angels are so desperate for a power hitter (right-handed, please), help in the bullpen, a catcher and possibly a shortstop, they are apparently willing to part with their lone drawing card.

Manager Dick Williams admits Nolan Ryan could be traded.

"We have no untouchables," said Williams.

That means The Express is available...and so are Mickey Rivers...Jerry Remy and Dave Collins, the club's hopes for the future.

Said Williams, "It is obvious that to get some quality people to strengthen our weaknesses, we are going to have to part with some quality talent.

"It is also rather obvious that on this team, most of it is in our starting pitching. We will have to take a long look before parting with our young players.

"But there is no untouchable on this club, to my line of thinking. How could there be? Have you taken a good look at the standings lately?"

Yes. The club is last in the American League West. Again.

General manager Harry Dalton was on his way to a meeting in New York and was unavailable for comment. Dalton has not been reluctant to deal top players in the past.

Dalton acquired Frank Robinson from Cincinnati (for Baltimore), traded him to the Dodgers, reacquired him for the Angels and then sent the future Hall of Famer to Cleveland.

The interleague swap session opens five days after the close of the World Series. The Angels initiated some trade talks at the All-Star meetings in Milwaukee.

"We're definitely going into the trade market this winter," he said. "We have to. We need punch, preferably from the right side, but I wouldn't turn down something from the left side."

Williams' team has hit only 13 home runs at home all season and 36 overall. The Angels are likely to wind up with the lowest American League total in more than two decades (55 by the 1954 Baltimore Orioles, the transplanted St. Louis Browns).

The super scouts have been called to Anaheim for meetings with Williams and Dalton.

"Yes, we're into things," said the manager. "There's a possibility a major trade could be made. We'll be meeting this homestand with our scouts who have been covering both leagues and will be talking to our coaches about possible deals.

"The way the races are greatly enhances our chances of making a major trade. You don't want somebody else's dirty wash and, by the same token, they don't want yours.

"We're laying the foundation for possible major deals. We haven't talked with other clubs at length, but we have a good idea what players on other teams will be moved."

Club president Arthur (Red) Patterson and general manager Dalton agreed with their field leader.

"For the first time in several years, we can package a deal, offering someone two or three players without robbing ourselves in another direction," said Dalton.

"We need a productive hitter. Power is fine, but RBIs are more important. Usually, you'll find those two items combined in one player."

Although Patterson stays out of the trading area except to be advised on what is happening, he also believes the Angels will make bold moves at the winter meetings in Hollywood, Florida. "I think we are going to have to," said Patterson. "We are going to have to give away some of our youngsters in order to make deals."

A FRUSTRATING YEAR FOR FIREBALLER RYAN

by DICK MILLER   **SEPTEMBER 27, 1975**

ANAHEIM—This is the kind of season it was for Nolan Ryan:

His big scene on television was approaching. Fans gathered around their sets to watch his appearance on a soap opera, "Ryan's Hope."

About all that had been visible of him earlier on the network show was the back of his head and his uncovered legs.

So what happened? Instead of the Angels pitcher, the face of the President of the United States appeared in the set.

A woman had tried to assassinate Gerald Ford.

"It's been some kind of year," sighed The Express.

He was sitting in the crowded living room of his rented Anaheim home. The room was filled with boxes as Nolan, Ruth and Reid Ryan packed to return home to Texas, three weeks before the end of the baseball season.

An orthopedic specialist, Dr. Joseph King, examined the bone chip in Ryan's pitching arm September 12 in Houston. Dr. King recommended surgery and the operation was scheduled September 23.

"Basically, the operation is the same one Jim Brewer had on his arm," Ryan said. "There are two bone chips. Dr. (Frank) Jobe told me I could begin throwing at 50 percent speed on December 1 if I agreed to have the operation now, but we really haven't mapped out a rehabilitation program yet."

How serious is the operation?

"Dr. Jobe says he can't guarantee it, but I should have a full recovery."

For most of his career, Ryan's talents have been compared with those of Sandy Koufax. Bothered by an arthritic elbow, Koufax called it a career prematurely at 31. Ryan is 28.

"I won't quit unless my arm falls off next spring," said Ryan. "The only way I can make this kind of money (an estimated $125,000 on the first year of a two-year contract) is to hold up a bank."

There is an eerie resemblance between the season Ryan has experienced and the torture Koufax went through for the Dodgers in 1962.

Koufax appeared in 28 games and won 14. Ryan has been in 28 games and won 14. Koufax pitched a no-hitter against the Mets in June and Ryan no-hit the Orioles in June.

Sandy pitched 11 complete games. The Dodger star missed more than two months of the season with an infected blister and a circulation blockage in the web of his pitching hand. He worked only 184⅓ innings.

Ryan has 10 complete games and will have missed about two months of the season with a succession of injuries. He has worked 198 innings. Koufax was the highest-paid Dodger player at $126,500. Ryan is the highest paid Angel player at $125,000.

The Express hopes to have as successful a comeback as Koufax. In 1963, Sandy won 25, lost only five and had an earned-run average of 1.88.

RYAN KEEPS ROLLING

N ot surprisingly, a few hundred strikeouts were now what everyone expected of Ryan. Speculation swirled of a 400-strikeout season, as well as 600 strikeouts and 60 victories for the Angels' pitching team of Ryan and Frank Tanana. In 1977, Ryan broke yet another of the immortal Sandy Koufax's records when he recorded his 98th game in which he fanned 10 or more batters. After being passed over by American League manager Billy Martin as a starting pitcher for the All-Star Game (Martin picked Tanana instead), Ryan refused to go as an "afterthought" pick when starters were injured and unable to play. As the season drew to a close, Ryan created more turmoil by criticizing Tanana, who sat out most of September with a sore arm, and some of the younger Angels for what he perceived as a lack of dedication to the team.

Ryan takes care of chores on his ranch in Alvin.

20 VICTORIES WOULD NOT SURPRISE RYAN

by DICK MILLER   **FEBRUARY 14, 1976**

ANAHEIM—Nolan Ryan should have felt good the morning of April 16, 1975. The day before, The Express had worked eight innings and gained credit for a 7-3 victory over the Twins. The season was only a week old and the Angels' righthander had a 3-0 pitching record.

When he awoke in his hotel room at the Leaminton Hotel, baseball's most overpowering pitcher realized his worst fear. His right arm, the one that made him strikeout king of the majors, a 20-game winner whose three no-hitters had raised him to the $125,000 salary class, was hurting.

Batters didn't know the tall Texan was injured. By May 18, he had an 8-1 record and the baseball authors were writing about a 30-victory season. He threw a no-hitter against the Orioles on June 1, his fourth, tying Sandy Koufax's record.

He appeared on the cover of *The Sporting News*, *Time* and *Sports Illustrated*. By June 6, Ryan had a 10-3 record. Half the victories were shutouts.

But it was all over for Ryan and his team. He lost his next eight decisions.

It can now be revealed Ryan accomplished all the shutouts, all the victories and the no-hitter with the painful arm injury that required off-season surgery and leaves him a question mark for 1976.

At the time, the media and fans were told Ryan had a calf muscle injury in his right leg, one that limited him to 11 innings of work in spring training.

"The leg injury wasn't as bad as people were led to believe," Ryan admitted. "But I definitely pulled the thing. It wasn't completely fictitious."

What does he expect in 1976?

"I don't know," he conceded. "Everyone is waiting to see. I've been throwing lightly for a while. I can't tell much. My arm feels just like it does in any other January.

"As usual, the shoulder bothers me more than anything else. The arm is as straight as I could ever get it. I have all the flexibility I've ever had."

Would he be surprised if he won 20 games this season?

"No."

Would he be surprised if he only won, say, five games?

"Yes. Very surprised."

Ryan said he doesn't know when he injured his arm. "I don't know for sure," he conceded. "I was most concerned after I pitched in Minnesota the first time up there. The next day, my arm was so sore I couldn't believe it."

By June, he knew surgery would be required to save his career.

"There's no way of telling how these things develop," he said in retrospect. "They actually were not bone chips. They were calcium deposits."

Bone chips and calcium deposits are common injuries for men who make their living throwing baseballs. One of Ryan's teammates, relief pitcher Jim Brewer, has had similar operations twice and still is pitching at 37.

Ryan talked about his injury.

"Calcium deposits come from strain where you have a little hemorrhaging in there. Blood coagulates to calcium size. Chips come from a blown elbow or where someone falls on his arm and actually chips part of the bone away.

"At least that is my understanding.

"Most pitchers you hear about who have bone chips actually have calcium deposits. People are misled to believe there actually is chipping of the bone."

Ryan estimates the scar on the outside of his right elbow is four to six inches long. No muscle had to be cut in the operation performed by Dr. Joseph King of Houston.

> Nolan and Ruth Ryan are the parents of a second boy, 7-pound, 2-ounce Nolan Reese Ryan, who will be known by his middle name. The Express' little choo choo is named after beloved Angel coach Jimmie Reese, Ryan's constant companion on the road.

RYAN RAPS PAY PREOCCUPATION

by MELVIN DURSLAG   **APRIL 24, 1976**

ANAHEIM—The sporting press brimmed with tales of high finance. Kareem Abdul-Jabbar was collecting everything but Wilshire Boulevard in Los Angeles. O.J. Simpson was asking Buffalo for Niagara Falls.

And, between them, Catfish Hunter and Joe Namath were earning enough to refinance New York City.

Generally described as baseball's most exciting pitcher, Nolan Ryan surveyed the scene calmly. According to reliable money-counters, he was working for a salary of roughly $125,000, which didn't reduce him to bread and water, but represented only laundry money in the context of what Andy Messersmith was seeking at the time.

Ryan was expressing the novel view that too many performers today are diluting their skills and decreasing their effectiveness because of overzealous occupation with pay.

"Don't get the idea I'm opposed to money," said Ryan, who has pitched four no-hitters for the Angels. "A man has to be paid for what he delivers. But once you get a respectable sum and keep pressing and pressing, you become unhappy, and soon money occupies more of your thoughts than your playing."

Nolan's listener tapped the side of his head to make sure the audio portion of this program was being heard correctly.

"Are you suggesting," he was asked, "that maybe athletes are overpaid?"

"I have read about baseball guys asking three and four hundred thousand dollars," he answered, "and I kind of laugh, because I've never seen a ballplayer worth even $250,000. Mays and Clemente might have been exceptions, but that's an awful lot of money for playing baseball."

Fearing for Nolan's life, we moved him into a corner and asked him to talk softer, lest word get back to the players and their guru, Marvin Miller.

But he continued with his philosophy, contend-ing that too many make the serious mistake of trying to get rich in sports.

"If a guy comes into sports at 22," said Nolan, "he is exceptional if he is around until he is 32. Most people are long gone before that. You shouldn't aim to get rich in such a short stretch. Sports just fills a brief period in your life, between the time you get out of school and the time you are ready to work at a normal job.

"During that span, you should try to make good money and maybe make connections that will help set you up in something afterward.

"But too many feel they should get rich, both in salary and on the side. It's too hard to do. Only a handful of guys have become rich in sports and zillions have driven themselves bugs trying."

As he talked, we had a vision of another good righthander by the name of Denny McLain, who became so engrossed with the proposition of making the world forget J. Paul Getty that he almost drove himself to the funny farm.

Even when he rose to his crest as a major league super star, shattering numberless records in the strikeout area, Ryan said he abandoned hope of getting wealthy in sports.

"You have to be in it mainly because you like it," he said, "and the best way to like it is to be good. Well, the only way to be good is to concentrate. You distract yourself with money arguments and with wheeling-and-dealing on the side and your playing has to suffer."

Ryan confessed frankly he never has cashed in on his four no-hitters and on all the records he has established.

"I have turned down a lot of business opportunities," he said, "and I rarely make speeches, even for pay. I do a few outside things, but I'm not bugged over money. I feel I have all I can do to keep my mind on conditioning and on pitching."

Ryan isn't a very conventional athlete. He doesn't even deal with the Angels through an agent, much less a lawyer, a CPA, an investment counselor and civil liberties advisor.

"After reading about the adventures of Messersmith," he was asked, "do you think you may alter your salary ideas if you have a good season in '76?"

"You have to base those things on the club's capability," he replied. "If we draw a lot of people, I would be inclined to ask for more.

"But whatever the negotiation, I would want it to be simple, because I don't like to bargain and I never expect to be the highest-paid player in baseball."

Raising our eyes and asking forgiveness for this young man who may have been suffering a recurrence of malaria or another form of delirium, we were advised further by Ryan that a number of athletes make a fetish over salary and fringe deals not because they are personally obsessed with money, but because their vanity is at stake.

Equating their skills only with the sum they are paid, they drive themselves bananas dredging banknotes from their targets.

This isn't good for the athlete in any endeavor, said Nolan, but it can be particularly distracting to a pitcher, mainly because pitching is such an inexact science.

"There is only one reason a pitcher has stuff one day and not the next," explained Ryan. "Whether the pitcher knows it or not, the mind will stray, for one reason or another, and he won't be able to throw the ball as he did the time before. Or often, he will have the same stuff, but because of concentration lapses, he won't be able to put the ball where he wants.

"Learning to pitch has been hard enough for me without additional handicaps. That's why I try to get a decent salary without muddling my mind with money fights."

Obviously, someone in the player's union must take Nolan aside for clinical talk. When a fellow mentioning pay speaks in terms of "the club's capability," it is a very dangerous precedent and he must be stopped.

Ryan is joined for a conference on the mound by manager Norm Sherry (center) and catcher Terry Humphrey.

ANGEL DUO COULD BE FIRST TO TOTAL 600 WHIFFS

by DICK MILLER　　　　**JULY 17, 1976**

ANAHEIM—It is a June night at Anaheim Stadium. The crowd stirs expectantly as Nolan Ryan walks out of the bullpen in the eighth inning for one of the few relief appearances of his career.

Awaiting him at home plate is Chicago's Dick Allen, on his way to becoming the Most Valuable Player in the American League.

Ryan walks down the slope of the mound to issue a challenge. "Hey, Dick, nothing but heat (fastballs)," the pitcher says.

"Right on!" Allen replies to the challenge.

It is a miniature drama that is played thousands of times a season. Few pitchers have the talent or guts of a Ryan to challenge a major league hitter in this manner. Maybe Allen is the only batter in the league who would joyously accept the challenge.

In this case it turns out to be a draw. Ryan doesn't strike out Allen and the batter doesn't get a hit. He flies to right field.

Ryan says he has struck out so many batters in his career (1,886) they no longer give him a thrill. His feeling was one of relief, not joy, when he fanned Minnesota's Rich Reese to break Sandy Koufax's single-season record in 1973.

Frank Tanana, his strikeout twin with the Angels, feels differently.

"A strikeout gives me the feeling of power, of strength, of being better than a hitter at that particular moment," said Tanana.

Ryan and Tanana, they are as different as, well, night and day. One is right-handed and famed for his fastball. Solid family man who is low-keyed.

The other is left-handed, feared most for his curveball. Solid swinger with bubbling personality.

They have one thing in common: the strikeouts. Together, they are on their way to becoming the first pitchers on the same team to record 300

strikeouts, the first modern-day pitchers in the American League to finish 1-2 in the majors in strikeouts.

Ryan leads with 128 and Tanana has 123. Both will be close to the 150 mark at the halfway point of the season.

"I think there is a very good chance we'll both get 300," said Tanana, who missed his last turn with a slight muscle pull in his pitching arm.

The pitching philosophies of Ryan and Tanana are as different as their temperaments and personalities. The Express throws over the top, Tanana across his body. "When I get two strikes on a batter, I try for a strikeout, no matter what the situation or score," said Tanana.

"I don't think Ryan cares about strikeouts," said Andy Etchebarren, who catches both.

"The only time I try for a strikeout is when a runner is in scoring position or if I have a big advantage in the count," said Ryan. "My best shot is if the count is 1-and-2. I can afford to waste a pitch.

"I think I've matured to the point where I don't get a special thrill from a strikeout any more."

Of his strikeout of Reese in his final game of 1973 that gave him 383 for the season and broke Koufax's record, he said:

"It was a feeling of relief more than anything else. It was the 13th inning, my leg was cramping and I was struggling. I knew I had thrown so many pitches I probably wouldn't get another start."

With Ryan injured, Tanana led the major leagues in strikeouts last season with 269. Ryan led both leagues the three previous years with 329 in 1972, 383 in '73 and 367 in 1974.

Only three times since the turn of the century have two pitchers from one club finished 1-2 in the majors in strikeouts.

Don Drysdale (232) and Koufax (216) did it for the Dodgers in 1962.

Way back in 1930, Lefty Grove (209) and George Earnshaw (193) were 1-2 for Connie Mack's Philadelphia A's. Further back in the infant days of the American League Rube Waddell (287) and Eddie Plank (210) also were 1-2 for Mack's 1905 A's.

What does it feel like to bat against the two pitchers?

"When he has a good day against me, I strike out three times," said five-time batting champion Rod Carew. "I crouch against Ryan because his ball rises. I try to hit it up the middle.

"He's improved a lot in the last couple of years with his curve and change. He's a great competitor. When you think he should be tiring, he rares back and fires, gets stronger in the seventh, eighth and ninth innings. And Tanana has come into his own."

Former American League home run king Bill Melton is glad to be on the same team with the pitchers. "Frank is an intelligent pitcher for 22 years old," he said. "His biggest asset is the control of his curve. He's the only left-handed pitcher I've seen in my eight years in the big leagues who can jam a right-handed hitter.

"Both are uncomfortable 0-for-4s. If Nollie is pitching good, he should throw the fastball 95 percent of the time. If he throws it low, it disappears. If he pitches you up, you can't hit it.

"When Nollie is pitching, most players sit on the bench to see how hard he is throwing."

Oddly, because of the way his ball moves, Tanana is more effective against right-handed hitters than lefthanders.

"Both are real easy to catch," said Etchebarren. "I've never caught a young pitcher like Tanana. His control is unbelievable.

"No one can approach Nollie for good stuff."

Ryan feeds cattle as he does chores around his home in Alvin, Texas.

RYAN EXPRESS NEARING 300 WHIFFS

by DICK MILLER   **OCTOBER 2, 1976**

ANAHEIM—Nolan Ryan is still as fast as Robert Feller.

And some nights he is as fast as Nolan Ryan.

The 2,000th strikeout of his career, in an 18-strikeout game against Chicago, and evidence offered by a sophisticated radar gun prove Ryan's arm is sound.

And that means The Express will be the subject of interesting trade talks this winter as the pitching-rich Angels try to improve their stricken hitting department.

"I may never see Holtville again," Ryan said at mid-season, and his overpowering performances in the closing weeks of the season may prove him correct. The Express recorded the 2,000th strikeout of his career (28 pitchers have done it) on September 1 against Detroit, then came back with an 18-strikeout performance against the White Sox on September 10.

That put him in a position to become the first pitcher in major league history to record 300 strikeouts in four seasons. With three starts remaining, he had 287.

Evidence that Ryan is as fast as ever was offered by a Ra-gun utilized by Texas scout Harley Anderson. A device used to clock pitchers' velocity by a number of scouts, it clocked Ryan's fastball at an average of 93 miles per hour with gusts up to 98 in the ninth inning. Anderson's gun clocked The Express' curve at 82 mph, slightly above the fastball of his pitching opponent that night, Detroit's Vern Ruhle.

Ryan might have been faster, but he had thrown in batting practice for 25 minutes the night before, expecting Frank Tanana to pitch.

When you consider that Ryan had thrown in batting practice the night before, it's apparent he is throwing as hard as when scientists from Rockwell International clocked him at 100.8 mph, breaking the formerly accepted mark of 98.6 by Feller.

"I haven't done much this year, so if I do get 300 strikeouts, that would be the highlight of my season," Ryan said.

Only two other pitchers have recorded three 300-strikeout seasons. Amos Rusie did it for the New York Giants from 1890 through '92, and Sandy Koufax for the L.A. Dodgers in 1963, '65 and '66.

Ryan is the only American League pitcher who has turned the trick, in three straight seasons beginning in 1972.

As this is written, Ryan has struck out 2,019 in 1,883 innings, a ratio that dwarfs the greats of the game. Walter Johnson, who leads in Ks, fanned 3,508 in 5,923 innings.

Next in total comes Bob Gibson, who in 17 years struck out 3,117 in 3,279 innings.

Koufax (in 12 years) is down the list with 2,396 strikeouts in 2,325, but excellent in his ratio of Ks to at-bats.

A private person, Ryan is willing to dive back into the fish bowl again to achieve his fifth no-hitter.

"My life has returned to normal," he said. "That means that I'm not achieving as much as I should. I happily would risk all the personal headaches again if I could throw a fifth no-hitter."

With the fastball gusting up to 100 mph again, there's always a chance.

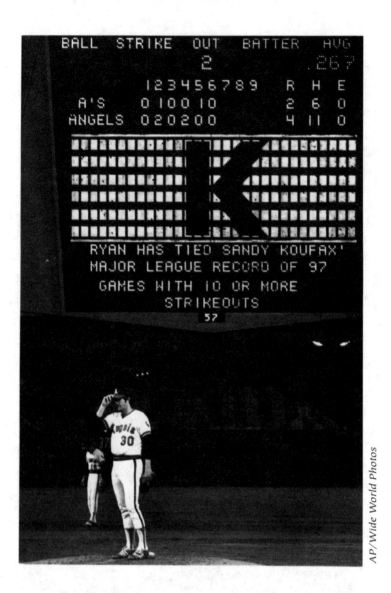

BALL STRIKE OUT BATTER AVG
2 .267

123456789 R H E
A'S   010010   2 6 0
ANGELS 020200   4 11 0

RYAN HAS TIED SANDY KOUFAX'
MAJOR LEAGUE RECORD OF 97
GAMES WITH 10 OR MORE
STRIKEOUTS
57

AP/Wide World Photos

RYAN-TANANA HILL TANDEM EYEING 60-VICTORY TARGET

by DICK MILLER   **JUNE 25, 1977**

ANAHEIM—Frank Tanana stood up as the Angels' team bus pulled up in front of the Sheraton-Centre Hotel in Toronto.

"All right you guys, get your rest tonight," he shouted. "Big game tomorrow."

Fast Frank turned to a writer and said, "Can you believe I said that? I'm not pitching."

It was Nolan Ryan's turn.

The two are baseball's version of the Odd Couple. They are as much alike as Alston and Lasorda, Koufax and Drysdale, McLain and Lolich.

Their only common denominator is on the pitching mound. Tanana was the major leagues' first nine-game winner. Ryan was an eight-game winner at the time.

Together, they are the hottest 1-2 pitching tandem baseball has seen since Sandy Koufax (26) and

Don Drysdale (23) combined for 49 Dodgers victories in 1966.

Tanana is ahead of Denny McLain's 31-victory pace of 1968. The Express is right behind him.

Ryan appears happy that Tanana has taken some of the media pressure off him. An intensely private man, Ryan has moved his family permanently from Alvin, Texas, to nearby Villa Park to escape the pressure of being a small-town celebrity.

"A celebrity can get lost in Southern California," said a friend. "There are a million of them. Nolan thinks he can get lost here. Back home they wanted him to preside over every banquet, clinic, fund raising and Little League opener."

Tanana loves the adulation of the masses. He is an extroverted bachelor, Ryan a dedicated family man. Between them, they are No. 1 and No. 2 in the American League in victories, strikeouts, games started, games completed and innings pitched.

There could be friction.

"Competition, if kept in the right context, is good," said Tanana. "There is nothing better in athletics than to have someone pushing you.

"Say Frank Tanana wants to be the best pitcher on the club. Ryan is having a great season. I have to have a spectacular season to be No. 1.

"That spurs me. It can work that way. I'd like to believe I don't need that to make me work hard. It does help. I view it that way."

Ryan likes to talk to people before pitching. He almost seems to seek out people for companionship. He'll talk about anything from baseball to business to Donk Reese's ice cream habit.

After the game, The Express is a difficult interview. He is much like Koufax. Polite, willing to talk but not willing to give much of himself to the reporters and radio people who gather around him.

Tanana comes from 180 degrees in the other direction.

He doesn't want to talk before a game. An intense competitor, he concentrates so hard on the game he almost ignores teammates and friends.

After a victory—his only losses this season came when the Angels were shut out at Boston and no-hit victims at Cleveland—Tanana is one of the best interviews in sports. He's articulate, a phrase-maker, candid and glib.

Before McLain, the last American League pitcher to win 31 games was Lefty Grove of the A's back in 1931. Donk Reese, 71 and the godfather of Reese Ryan, 1, played with Grove and now conditions Angel pitchers.

Ryan thinks it will be difficult for either to reach the 30-victory plateau.

"We'll be in five-man rotation at times," he pointed out.

Another difference: Ryan prefers to work with three days' rest and throws about 150 pitches a game. Tanana prefers to work every fifth day and requires only about 100 pitches.

Ryan was averaging 9.78 srikeouts a game and was holding batsmen to a composite .181 average. Tanana was striking out 8.61 batters per nine innings and holding the hitters to a .218 average.

Despite their fast starts, the Ryan-Tanana combo is unlikely to set a record for combined wins. Iron Man Joe McGinnity (35) and Christy Mathewson (33) set the major league standard of 68 for the 1904 New York Giants. That same year, Jack Chesbro (41) and John Powell (23) won 64 for the New York American League Club.

Lolich added only 17 wins to McLain's 31 in 1968. Another Tiger pair, Prince Hal Newhouser (29) and Paul Dizzy Trout (27) had 56 wins in 1944.

Paul (Daffy) Dean failed to win 20 games when Dizzy went 30-7 in 1934. Boston had a great combination in 1949 in Mel Parnell (25) and Ellis Kinder (23).

ANGEL NOTEBOOK: In his book to be published soon, Ryan will confess to cheating occasionally to record a strikeout. He has thrown his 100 mph fastball from as much as a foot in front of the pitching rubber. Since everyone else in baseball cheats, Ryan cheerfully confesses he does in "The Other Game," written by Bill Libby, the one-man Book of the Month Club. "You can do it on certain mounds," Ryan revealed. "I can cheat six inches to a foot. I dig a trench in front of the mound a couple of innings in advance. . . Cheating is accepted in baseball so I participated."

400 WHIFFS? RYAN MAY DO IT DESPITE ACHING ARM

by DICK MILLER   **JULY 9, 1977**

ANAHEIM—How long will Nolan Ryan's pitching arm last if he continues to throw 170 pitches a game?

The Express doesn't pretend to have the answer. His arm hurt him so much after loosening up, he had to take a pain killer. So 48 hours later, he struck out 19 Toronto batters in 10 innings of a 13-inning game, during which he retired the first 16 Blue Jays in succession. He could have gone another inning and broken Tom Cheney's record of 21 strikeouts in a single game. Manager Norm Sherry wisely didn't give him a chance after Ryan had thrown 171 pitches.

In his next start, he had thrown 139 pitches by the seventh inning and Sherry took him out with the club holding a commanding lead.

"My arm is tired. It's dead," The Express admitted.

That's good news for American League hitters.

The bad news is that's the same way his arm felt in 1973 when he broke Sandy Koufax's record with 383 strikeouts. With barely a third of the season completed, Ryan already had 176 strikeouts.

"I've pitched with a bad arm before," said Ryan. "I don't want any extra rest. I want to pitch every fourth day. I feel I have to for this team to win. It's the first time we've ever had a chance to win a pennant."

Perhaps no mortal ever has thrown a baseball more effectively than Ryan did in his first seven innings against the Blue Jays. For only the third time in his career, he went into the eighth inning without issuing a walk.

So how did Ryan feel about his performance?

"No one was more surprised than I was," he admitted.

"I had thrown longer than normal in the bullpen Monday working on my delivery. When I finished, my arm was throbbing. I had to go to the clubhouse and take something for the pain.

"It felt like a toothache."

If Ryan is able to get 40 starts in—he had to get an extra day off earlier in the season after making 197 pitches in a game—he could surpass 400 strikeouts for the season.

He's a better pitcher than in 1973 when he went down to the final pitch of his last start to break Koufax' record.

He has remained ahead of his '73 pace for strikeouts.

Barring a bionic implant, will The Express' arm make it through the summer?

"I don't know," he admitted.

His teammates could save a lot of wear and tear on Ryan's arm if they would support him more often as they did against Cleveland recently. Two home runs by Joe Rudi, good for five runs batted in, and home runs off the bats of Dave Chalk and Don Baylor enabled Sherry to take Ryan out of the Cleveland game early.

Ryan rushes to trainer Freddie Frederico's room after every start. His right arm and shoulder are packed in ice for 15 or 20 minutes.

"You never required that much ice before," it was pointed out.

"My arm was never 30 years old before," he replied with a smile.

Ryan appears faster now than when his fastball was timed at 100.9 miles per hour. His curve has never been better. And for 10 magic innings against Toronto, his control was pinpoint. "When he missed, it was only by an inch," said catcher Andy Etchebarren.

That's the way Sandy Koufax and Bob Feller were at their best.

Ryan has struck out 19 batters three times. It's a feat that has been performed only 10 times in major league history. He wanted a shot at Cheney's record, set in a 16-inning game against Baltimore in 1962.

Ryan displays the ball with which he struck out Bill Stein, giving him the record for games with 10 or more strikeouts.

AP/Wide World Photos

"I wanted to go another inning," he admitted. "I left it up to Norman. It turned out he was right (the Angels didn't score in the 11th inning).

"The last two innings, I didn't have as good velocity as earlier. I didn't think I had that much of a chance at a record."

Shortstop Bobby Grich, who hit the game-winning, 13th-inning home run, summed up a lot of players' feelings:

"When Nolan is pitching, I feel like I should pay my way into the ball park.

"I'm a spectator."

"NEVER AGAIN," SAYS RYAN OF "AFTERTHOUGHT" PICK

by DICK MILLER   **AUGUST 6, 1977**

ANAHEIM—Nolan Ryan of the Angels was charged with a balk as the result of his refusal to join the American League All-Star squad.

Billy Martin of the Yankees, manager of the American League All-Stars, picked The Express to replace injured Frank Tanana on the A.L. pitching staff.

Martin expected Ryan to start.

"It's an honor to be picked," said Ryan. "But it will be hard to start under the circumstances. I'll be soaking up the sun at Laguna Beach."

Ryan meant what he said. While the A.L. was absorbing a 7-5 All-Star beating, he was home in California.

Ryan's pride was injured when Martin passed him over in the original selections. And who could blame Ryan?

At the time the All-Star hurlers were picked, Nolan's 12 victories tied him for the major league lead with Tanana and the Cubs' Rick Reuschel. Ryan led the majors with 222 strikeouts and his 2.58 ERA was among the lowest in either league among the starting pitchers.

And in his last start before the All-Star break, Nolan notched win No. 13 and topped one of Sandy Koufax's most impressive records. In defeating the Mariners, 5-4, July 16, while fanning 12, Ryan passed Koufax by posting his 98th game with 10 or more strikeouts.

"If I can't go on my merits the first time around (with the original selections) I'm not going," Nolan declared.

"I threw two no-hitters in 1973 and wasn't picked. It caused such a big stink the commissioner

> ## "If I can't go on my merits the first time around (with the original selections) I'm not going," Nolan declared.

(Bowie Kuhn) added a player to each team.

"Willie Mays went for the National League and I went for the American League. That was the last time I'll go under any circumstances other than being picked on the first go-around."

The American League's three top pitchers—Ryan, Tanana and Detroit's Mark Fidrych—missed the game with injuries. The A.L. went down to its sixth straight loss and 14th in 15 years.

Martin blamed the selection process for forcing him to pass up Ryan in his original selections. But he did select reliever Dave LaRoche of the Angels, along with Tanana.

Under the rules the fans pick the starting line-ups in nationwide voting. The two managers select the starting pitchers and reserves. Every team must be represented by at least one player.

"The selection process paints you into a corner," said Martin. "I took Vida Blue off the Oakland roster and Jim Kern from Cleveland.

"When I came to the Angels, from a starting standpoint Tanana was having a better year than Ryan. On the basis of relief, I picked LaRoche.

"I have nothing personal against Ryan. I like the guy very much. He's been one of the best pitchers I've seen in years."

Ryan's teammates were shocked at the gross oversight.

"I can't believe it," said Tanana.

"There were only two 12-game winners in the American League. It's just unbelievable that he couldn't be on the team. He has the third or fourth best ERA in the league for starting pitchers."

Said LaRoche, who pitched one shutout inning in the All-Star Game, "The way I started the season in Cleveland, I had no thought about making the team. It's an honor. I'm disappointed for some of my teammates like Bobby Bonds, Dave Chalk, Jerry Remy and Ryan."

Not even a personal phone call from American League president Lee MacPhail could convince Ryan to change his mind.

MacPhail telephoned Ryan personally after hearing that the major league strikeout king had refused to play because he was selected as an "afterthought."

"I told him I understood his reasons but I urged him to change his mind. I told him I thought it was in the best interests of the American League, himself and baseball as a whole that he play in the game," said MacPhail.

"I told him to take an hour and reconsider. I said, 'After that hour, if you've changed your mind, call me back.' He didn't call back. It was his deci-

sion. A player doesn't have to play in the All-Star Game if he doesn't want to. There's no stipulation in the contract."

Don Sutton of the Dodgers, who started for the National League, and was named the game's MVP, said he felt anyone should be proud to represent his league in the All-Star Game, but said he respected Ryan's honesty.

"Ballplayers have a tendency to tell people what they want to hear rather than the truth," said Sutton. "I admire Nolan's honesty. In his position, I might have done the same thing."

And Jim Palmer, who started for the A.L. and was bombed for three home runs, said before the game that he felt Ryan should have been the starting A.L. pitcher. Refusing to blame Ryan or Martin, Palmer said he thought 10 or 12 pitchers should be selected instead of the usual seven or eight.

NOTHING PERSONAL, RYAN BELIEVES

by *MELVIN DURSLAG*   **AUGUST 16, 1977**

ANAHEIM—Assuming that he would be an original selection to the American League team in the All-Star Game, Nolan Ryan made reservations to New York for himself, his wife and their oldest son, who would be seeing the Statue of Liberty and other landmarks of Manhattan for the first time.

The family had made arrangements to visit close friends in Greenwich—people by the name of Seaver. Mr. Seaver's firm had transferred him to Cincinnati, but he kept the home in Connecticut.

It was logical for Ryan to believe that Billy Martin, the manager of the American Leaguers, would select him, considering that Ryan was one of only two pitchers to win 12 games at the time.

Not long before, for the 97th time, he had consummated the task of striking out 10 or more batters in a game, matching the record of Sandy Koufax.

And if other credentials were to be weighed, Ryan had pitched four no-hitters. In the past, only

Koufax did that.

Since Sandy entered the Hall of Fame on the first vote—a rare achievement—the feeling began to grow that what Ryan was doing in baseball wasn't frivolous.

But Bill Martin isn't easily impressed. He didn't pick Ryan until his first selections developed injuries, paving the way for the following:

(a) Ryan told him to stuff it and (b) he went out and fanned 10 or more for the 98th time, breaking Koufax's record.

Reflecting on the All-Star affair, Ryan questions Martin's judgment, but he doesn't feel Billy bypasses him for personal reasons.

"Have you ever tangled with Martin before?" Nolan was asked.

"Probably no more than other pitchers have," he responded. "When he was at Detroit, he did a lot of bench jockeying while I was on the mound. He's the worst needler in baseball. He also stopped the game one day and questioned a hole in my shirt. He yelled that it was distracting the hitters and he got the umpire to make me change it."

"Did he ever do anything more serious?"

"When he moved to the Rangers, I went out to the mound there and found a big snake. It turned out to be one of those rubber snakes, but it was supposed to unnerve me and we suspected Billy."

Obviously, Martin forgot that Ryan comes from Texas and Texans don't run scared of snakes, especially Nolan, who has seen more rattlers than he has Italian managers.

"I choose to believe Billy does these things because of competitiveness," said Ryan, "and not for personal reasons. And I doubt that he passed me in the All-Star Game for any personal reasons."

NOLAN RYAN'S CAREER ALL-STAR STATISTICS

Year	Club	W	L	ERA	G	GS	CG	SH	IP	H	R	ER	BB	SO
1972	California (AL)	Did not play												
1973	California (AL)	0	0	9.00	1	0	0	0	2.0	2	2	2	2	2
1975	California (AL)	Did not play												
1979	California (AL)	0	0	13.50	1	1	0	0	2.0	5	3	3	1	2
1981	Houston (NL)	0	0	0.00	1	0	0	0	1.0	0	0	0	0	1
1985	Houston (NL)	0	0	0.00	1	0	0	0	3.0	2	0	0	2	2
1989	Texas (AL)	1	0	0.00	1	0	0	0	2.0	1	0	0	0	3
	AL Totals	1	0	7.50	3	1	0	0	6.0	8	5	5	3	7
	NL Totals	0	0	0.00	2	0	0	0	4.0	2	0	0	2	3
	Totals	1	0	4.50	5	1	0	0	10.0	10	5	5	5	10

MARTIN WRITES OFF RYAN EARLY

By Dick Miller   January 14, 1978

ANAHEIM—Nolan Ryan won't be on the American League All-Star team in 1978. This time it won't be the Angel pitcher's idea.

"I want you to print this," said Yankee manager Billy Martin. "I won't pick Ryan if he's won 40 games by the All-Star break. He can kiss my petunia."

The manager of the world champions, who will guide the American League squad in the '78 classic at San Diego, is still upset over Ryan's refusal to accept a bid last year. Martin originally picked Ryan's teammate, Frank Tanana, along with another Angel, reliever Dave LaRoche.

When Tanana was forced to skip the game due to an arm injury, Martin switched to Ryan and said he would be starting against the National League. Ryan said he wouldn't go.

American League president Lee MacPhail may have to intervene in the case next July.

RYAN, TANANA EYEING CY YOUNG PRIZE

by DICK MILLER   **SEPTEMBER 10, 1977**

ANAHEIM—In 1973, Nolan Ryan tossed two no-hitters, barely missed a third, broke Sandy Koufax's season strikeout record and won 21 games for a last-place team.

He finished second to Baltimore's Jim Palmer in the American League Cy Young balloting. Palmer won 22 games for a division winner.

"I learned a long time ago there is no justice in baseball," Ryan said recently. "I won't even think about the award until the season is over."

In 1976, Palmer again won the Cy Young Award. His 22-13 record was nine games over .500 for a contender, the same as Frank Tanana's 19-10 mark for California. Detroit's Mark Fidrych was 10 games over .500 at 19-9.

Backed by an atrocious defensive club, Tanana still managed a better earned-run average than Palmer, 2.44 to 2.51. Tanana said after the vote was in, "It's like Catfish Hunter said, 'With Palmer, it's Cy or cryin'.'"

Prediction: The American League is headed for another controversy in its Academy Awards for the pitching arts.

Again, smack in the middle are Ryan and Tanana.

The villains in this piece again will be veterans of the Baseball Writers' Association of America, who certainly have a better voting system than what is used for the Heisman Trophy and John R. Wooden Awards. They don't always use it wisely.

Unlike the Heisman voting, where the prep writer for the *Porterville Gazette* has as much power as writers for major papers who travel the college football circuit, there are only two voters in each league city, or 28 American League Cy Young voters.

Generally, they are the traveling writers who see between 140 and 162 games a season, not counting spring training. They vote for three pitchers on a 10-5-1 point basis.

The Baseball Writers' Association hasn't defined the criteria for the Cy Young Award—or for the Most Valuable Player Award. And that's the problem.

From a pitcher's viewpoint, what are the qualifications for the award symbolic of the league's top pitcher?

"It's an honor," said Ryan. "The voters shouldn't be concerned if he got shafted the year before.

"They should look at the merits of his statistics. First, they should look at his contribution to the club. And then his consistency throughout the year.

"I'd look at his starts, complete games, wins, innings pitched, hits given up, strikeouts and earned-run average.

"You have to analyze a guy's record. Does an 8-7 win for a guy pitching for the Yankees mean the same as a guy losing a 2-6 game for Oakland?

"I don't think you can put this kind of information into a computer and come out with an answer. When I was with the Mets, Houston wanted a left-handed relief pitcher.

"They fed the names of all the pitchers they thought were available into a computer with all the information that was available about them. They came out with the name of Jack DiLaurio of the Mets. He was supposed to be the most effective lefthander available.

"They got him in mid-season. And he wasn't even with the club the next year."

Ryan recently was the only 17-game winner, but The Express is seven games over .500, the same as teammate Frank Tanana at 14-7.

RYAN BREAKS ANGELIC PEACE BY RAPPING TANANA

by DICK MILLER   **OCTOBER 1, 1977**

ANAHEIM—Nolan Ryan's image as the silent Texan will have to undergo an overhaul now that he has criticized teammate Frank Tanana and some of the Angels' younger players.

"I'm getting tired of people using me as an excuse," Ryan said 24 hours after it was announced that Tanana's tired arm would require a rest, perhaps for the season.

"If it isn't one thing, it's another," said Ryan. "I'm being made to feel like the scapegoat for Frank's arm and I don't want it that way."

Tanana had said his arm was tired from overwork and that he was incapable of pitching 300 innings a season. But at no time had he put the blame on Ryan.

Ryan prefers to work every fourth day to maintain his rhythm. Tanana, Ken Brett, Gary Ross and Wayne Simpson among the other starters prefer five-day rotations.

"I don't know why he feels so guilty," Tanana said. "I never meant to imply that he is the reason for my sore arm. There is no way I meant to insinuate that was the case. But he can say what he wants."

The bad feelings between the pitchers came as a surprise.

"I read where Frank says he will refuse to pitch unless it's every fifth day," said Ryan. "What if I were to refuse to pitch unless it was every fourth day?"

Ryan jabbed the needle home.

"As far as I'm concerned, he hasn't worked hard or pushed himself since the All-Star break," Ryan said. "At least that is my observation."

Tanana replied, "It's his observation and I'm not going to push the issue. I just don't know why he wants to knock."

While admiring Tanana's work as a professional craftsman, Ryan said, "He can be one of the best pitchers in baseball and, when he is on the mound, there's nobody who is more competitive. But there is more to it than just going out there every four or five days and throwing a baseball.

"You have to prepare yourself physically and mentally. It seems to me that winning has become secondary to a lot of players, mostly the younger ones. They're more concerned with how much money they're making and how to prolong their careers."

Ryan, who once said he would like to pitch every third day, is resigned to pitching in a five-man rotation next season.

"I always felt I performed better in a four-man rotation, but if the rest can't go, then we'll have to go on a five-man rotation," he said.

After delaying a decision until September 9, the Angels finally announced that Tanana would rest his ailing arm for 10 days, a span that was expected to stretch into the remainder of the season.

Fast Frank's arm began to hurt him on June 10 when he had a 10-2 record and 1.84 ERA. It forced him to withdraw from the All-Star Game.

With 10 miles an hour gone from his fastball and unable to throw more than five or six curves a game, Tanana saw his record drop to 15-9 and his ERA jump to 2.54. It probably cost him the American League Cy Young Award.

Said Tanana, "If I pitch every fifth day, I'm fully capable of going nine innings every time out. I can give you a solid 250, 260, 270 innings a season. Three hundred may be over my physical capabilities."

RYAN WALKAWAY WINNER AS TOP A.L. PITCHER

by DICK MILLER   **OCTOBER 22, 1977**

ANAHEIM—A subject for debate: how much do walks count in a pitcher's performance? "Any pitcher who walks 200 batters in a season doesn't deserve the Cy Young Award," said Baltimore's Jim Palmer.

"It doesn't matter how many you walk just as long as they don't score," countered California's Nolan Ryan, baseball's leading expert on walks.

American League players apparently agree with Ryan. He was voted the league's Pitcher of the Year in a player poll conducted by *The Sporting News.*

The results were overwhelming. Ryan received 110 votes with Minnesota's Dave Goltz second at 36 and the Angels' Frank Tanana third with 34.

Palmer, who made a late-season surge to become one of the American League's three 20-game winners, finished well down in voting.

"I'm glad Jim Palmer isn't voting for the Cy Young Award," said Ryan's wife, Ruth.

As the A.L.'s No. 1 hurler, Ryan will receive an engraved Bulova Accuquartz wrist watch.

The award is likely to be shrouded in controversy. Ryan, always a powerful finisher, came up with a sore arm in September and finished with a 9-16 record and was third among starting pitchers with a 2.77 earned-run average.

Only Tanana and Texas' Bert Blyleven finished ahead of The Express. Ryan also led the majors with 22 complete games, 341 strikeouts and 204 walks, missing Bob Feller's modern record by four when he was unable to make the last trip of the season.

"I don't really expect to win the Cy Young Award," said Ryan, who was advised early in September to rest his arm for the remainder of the season.

He started against Kansas City on September 25, but his arm began to tighten in the third inning and he had to be relieved in the seventh with the score tied at 2-2 and two runners on base.

A line drive that was lost in the sun off reliever Dave LaRoche went as a triple and Ryan was charged with the loss.

"*The Sporting News* award means a lot to me because it is from the players," Ryan said before returning to his home in Alvin, Texas.

A few days before, he had picked up a newspaper and read this comment from Palmer: "I think I deserve the Cy Young Award. A pitcher who walks 200 batters doesn't deserve it."

"I won't blast him," Ryan countered. "He's just worried someone can beat him out of the award. He likes to pick out things.

"It doesn't matter how many you walk just so long as they don't score. (Ryan's ERA was 2.77, Palmer's 2.91.)

"He made the comment in 1973 that I went for strikeouts and he went for outs.

"Aren't they the same? I don't think the manager cares how you get them out just so long as you do."

Palmer was *The Sporting News*' Pitcher of the Year and the Cy Young Award winner in 1973 with a 22-9 record for a Baltimore team that won its division by eight games.

Ryan was 21-16, broke Sandy Koufax's single-season strikeout record, tossed two no-hitters and a one-hitter, and didn't win an award while working for a team that finished 15 games out of first place.

There is no love lost between the Angels' pitchers and Palmer.

"It's like Catfish Hunter says," commented Tanana, "With Palmer it's Cy or cryin'."

Ryan seldom has had the luxury of working with a big lead. But once he has a late lead, look out. He's death. As an Angel, he is 86-2, with three no-decisions, in games in which he was given a lead through seven innings. He completed 74 of those games. Here's a year-by-year breakdown of that fantastic 86-2 record: In 1972, it was 14-0; in '73, 17-0; in '74, 18-2 with one no-decision; in '75, 10-0 and one no-decision; in '76, 15-0 with one no-decision; and the past season it was 12-0. "I only had one laugher after the All-Star break," Ryan pointed out. "The mental wear and tear was the worst I've ever been through. I had the feeling if I gave up a run I'd lose."

The Express made 14 starts after the All-Star break. The Angels scored 39 runs for him in 11 weeks. His team-mates backed him up with seven, six and six runs in three of those starts and he won each game. In the 11 other starts, they scored a total of 20 runs for him.

These are some of Ryan's 1977 accomplishments the players took into consideration:

-Became the first pitcher in history to have five 300-plus strikeout seasons.

-Recorded fourth 19-strikeout game of his career June 8 against Toronto.

-The league's cumulative batting average against Ryan was .190.

-Struck out 10 or more batters in a game 20 times. It extended his major league record to 104. Koufax held the old mark at 97.

-Moved ahead of Koufax into the No. 15 spot on the all-time strikeout list with 2,426.

-His 341 strikeouts are No. 6 on the single-season list. Ryan also is No. 1, 3, 7 and 8.

The stiffness in Ryan's right forearm is muscular and isn't believed to be serious. "I see no reason why I can't pitch another four years," he said.

"Unless I have an injury, I see no reason to change my pitching style. I won't work on new pitches next spring because I don't think I need any.

"The biggest thing is for me to cut down on walks and reduce the game tension they cause. My speed is the same as it's always been as far as I can detect."

The Angels finished 14 games out of first place

in 1976. Gene Autry spent $5.2 million to sign free agents Joe Rudi, Bobby Grich and Don Baylor and another $2 million in long-term contracts and cash to Cleveland and Chicago for pitchers Dave LaRoche and Ken Brett.

So the Angels finished twice as far behind, 28 games.

"It's been the most frustrating year of my life," said Ryan. "I'm going home and try to forget it."

There was one highlight as far as Ryan was concerned.

"I feel I found consistency. I only had one terrible game (in 37 starts) when I was taken out in the third or fourth inning at Texas."

Ryan just missed working 300 innings for the third time in his career. He finished with 299, but still prefers to work every fourth day while Tanana and the remainder of the staff prefer four days off between starts.

Palmer, the Royals' Dennis Leonard and the Twins' Dave Goltz made the 20-win level in the final week of the season. Since Cy Young won 31 games in 1901, there have been only three years in American League history there wasn't a 20-game winner.

"It looks like the National League is going to wind up with all the 20-game winners," Ryan admitted.

"Managers are going to have to take starters out in the seventh inning if they have a substantial lead and they have the kind of bullpen which affords them a chance to make a change.

"More and more pitchers are getting tired late in the season. I'd help myself if I would cut off 20 or 30 pitches a game."

Ryan averages about 150 pitches a game. In 1973, coach Jimmie Reese's chart had Ryan throwing 7,500 pitches.

What's ahead for Ryan and the jinxed Angels?

"Next year, everyone will be healthy so we will have a good defense. The club went bad this year and I don't know why. Everyone was so optimistic. It reached the point where we didn't come out of it."

> "Unless I have an injury, I see no reason to change my pitching style. I won't work on new pitches next spring because I don't think I need any. The biggest thing is for me to cut down on walks and reduce the game tension they cause. My speed is the same as it's always been as far as I can detect."

In a 1977 poll conducted by *The Sporting News,* the American League players voted Ryan the league's Pitcher of the Year.

LEAVING CALIFORNIA

NOLAN RYAN

R yan's dominance continued even as he passed his 30th birthday. In 1978, he passed Bob Feller and Warren Spahn to move into eighth place on the career strikeouts list. Based on his season average, he was expected to move into fourth place during 1979, and second during 1980. As Opening Day of the 1979 season approached, Ryan told the Angels he would become a free agent if he did not have a new contract before the season started. He wasn't bluffing; in November, he signed a three-year deal with the team in his own backyard, the Houston Astros.

AP/Wide World Photos

RYAN'S FUTURE AT STAKE IN STRETCH RUN

by DICK MILLER   **AUGUST 19, 1978**

ANAHEIM—The closing weeks of the 1978 season will be crucial to Nolan Ryan's future. Some time next winter, The Express will decide whether he will request a trade to the Rangers and possibly whether he will retire following the 1979 season.

"If the Angels make a sincere run at the pennant, I'd like to come back here," Ryan said while he was passing Bob Feller and Warren Spahn and moving into the No. 8 spot on baseball's all-time strikeout list.

Ryan always has insisted he wasn't hung up on longevity, although every season he pitches probably is worth $250,000 to him, plus another year in the pension plan.

He also insists records mean nothing to him, but they could be a deciding factor when he finishes out his three-year contract next season.

With what is left of this season and his normal 300 strikeouts in '79 he could pass his friend Tom Seaver, Mickey Lolich, Cy Young, and Jim Bunning and move into the No. 4 spot behind Walter Johnson, Bob Gibson and Gaylord Perry.

With just another year beyond that, Ryan could move into the No. 2 spot at the relatively young age of 33, with a good chance of passing Johnson.

Ryan passed Spahn on August 2 when he struck out eight Oakland batters in a 1-0 loss to the A's. He also reclaimed the American League strikeout lead that night from the Yankees' Ron Guidry, 164 to 163.

Ryan had an interesting thought about strikeout pitchers:

"I wonder if any of the guys on the all-time strikeout list ever had an arm operation? I don't think guys in the early history of the game like Walter Johnson or Cy Young did.

"When I had mine in the winter of 1975, the doctor wasn't optimistic. All he said was, 'I've seen worse arms.' He didn't say, 'You'll be as good as new.'

"I didn't know what to expect."

How long can he continue to throw bullets?

"Only the Lord knows," Ryan said with a smile. "When I was in Las Vegas for a 'Sports Challenge' taping a couple of months ago, Bob Feller told me, 'I don't see how you can still throw so hard at your age.'

"I didn't know if I should take that as a compliment at 31."

The Express continues to insist he doesn't get any special kick out of a strikeout or the numbers. "The only thing it means," he said, "is that I've taken good stuff out there. And I've maintained my stuff over the years."

Ryan shows no sign of slowing down, of becoming a junk-ball pitcher in his 30s.

"My fastball is as good as ever, except I don't burn it as much as I used to because I don't have to. I threw a pitch to Eric Soderholm this season that was probably the hardest I've ever thrown. I felt my motion, everything going together."

Feller spent nearly four years in the military service and Spahn also lost three years.

"That probably cost Feller 1,000 strikeouts," said Ryan. "He could have been second on the all-time list. I saw Spahn later in his career. By then he was a crafty lefthander."

"Crafty" is a player's description of a pitcher who pitches with his head, not only with his arm.

Ryan is now 31, the age at which Sandy Koufax, the Dodger great, retired. He has one year remaining on a three-year contract and has no idea how long he will continue to pitch.

Koufax was forced into a premature retirement by fears that pitching would cause him permanent damage with acute arthritis.

Ryan's arm, by contrast, shows no sign of abuse. Even the surgical scar on his elbow appears to be only a small nick.

RYAN TO ANGELS: RE-SIGN ME BY APRIL 4, OR—

by DICK MILLER   **November 18, 1978**

ANAHEIM—Nolan Ryan's fabled fastball shows little sign of slowing down. In one test last season, using the same radar gun used by law enforcement officials to clock speeding cars, the 31-year-old Ryan's fastball was clocked at 96 mph and his curve at 82 mph.

The Express, who has always maintained, "I have no hangup over how long my career lasts," has decided he will pitch for another five years.

"I'll pitch as long as I'm physically able and want to," Ryan said in explaining a contract offer to general manager Buzzie Bavasi.

Ryan's current three-year contract terminates in 1979, at which time he will be eligible to become a free agent.

The righthander has offered to extend his current contract four more years, which would take him through 1983.

"I'm just trying to cover the maximum number of years I want to pitch," Ryan said from his winter home in Alvin, Texas. He also owns a home in Villa Park near Anaheim Stadium. "At the end of the season, I sent Buzzie a letter setting down some of my thoughts."

The letter also included an authorization to trade him to either the Rangers or Astros. The offer expires on December 15.

"The club (Angels) has been good to me," said Ryan. "I'm offering them a chance to extend my contract. I want to sign my last contract with maybe an option year."

Although Ryan finished with only a 10-13 record, he threw extremely well after the All-Star Game and won his sixth American League strikeout title despite Ron Guidry's big year and Nolan's two injuries.

If Ryan can bounce back with another 20-victory season and register a record fifth no-hitter, how much would he be worth as a free agent?

Start at a million dollars even if he will be 32. Although they are different types of pitchers, Gaylord Perry still is going strong at 40 and might have won a pennant for the Rangers if he hadn't been traded to San Diego.

Ryan says 1979 will be his final season with the Angels if details of a new contract aren't worked out by the season opener April 4.

"I don't want to negotiate a contract through the season," he said. "I've seen how that bothers some players."

Dick Moss, the former counsel for Marvin Miller and the Major League Players Association, has been hired by Ryan to handle the negotiations.

ANGELS' NOTEBOOK: In a surprise move, Larry Sherry was hired as the Angels' pitching coach on October 30...Marv Grissom had been invited to return by Jim Fregosi, but was unable to reach terms with general manager Buzzie Bavasi. Sherry had resigned as Pittsburgh's pitching coach to spend more time at his Mission Viejo home, which is a block away from Norm Sherry, the former Angels' manager. Sherry and Fregosi had shared a motel room in Pittsburgh early in the season when Fregosi was a part-time player for the Pirates...Hired along with Sherry were Bobby Knoop and Deron Johnson. Knoop, who reportedly also had a job offer from the Yankees, will coach at first base. He was the White Sox' third base coach last season. A longtime major leaguer, Johnson will be the batting instructor, replacing Bob Skinner, who went to Pittsburgh. He managed Salt Lake City (PCL) last season.

NEW PACT BY OPENING DAY OR FREE AGENCY, SAYS RYAN

by DICK MILLER   **MARCH 10, 1979**

PALM SPRINGS—Nolan Ryan, with four no-hitters, baseball's single-season strikeout record and six major league strikeout titles to his credit, checked into the Angels' spring training headquarters for what might be the final time. Entering his eighth season as an Angel and the final season of a three-year contract, Ryan said he will test the free-agent market next fall if he hasn't signed a new agreement by opening day.

Negotiations between Ryan and California general manager Buzzie Bavasi are cordial and Ryan says he hopes to remain with the Angels.

With Ryan coming off a 10-13 season at the age of 32, the Angels are reluctant to offer their superstar pitcher a multi-year contract believed to call for about $2 million.

"I can understand their point," Ryan said. "But I've made it very clear I'm not going to go through any form of negotiations during the season."

It has been learned that Ryan's agent, Richard Moss, came close to asking commissioner Bowie Kuhn to declare the pitcher a free agent last month because Ryan had made an oral agreement with former G.M. Harry Dalton that gave Ryan a $50,000 advance on his salary each year before going to spring training.

When Bavasi refused to honor the agreement, Moss threatened to seek free agency.

The $50,000 was paid.

"I'm not upset with Nollie at all," Bavasi said. "I'm upset with his agent, not because he may become a free agent but for asking for his free agency because we didn't send him a $50,000 check in advance.

"I'm annoyed by that. There's nothing in writing, nothing in the contract. You are not allowed to do anything unless it is in the contract. It is a violation to give a player a nickel more than is in the contract."

If Ryan becomes a free agent in October the Angels plan to file a claim for him in the reentry draft. Ryan says he would consider signing with the Angels again as a free agent. "I have no burning desire to leave Anaheim," he said after moving into his Villa Park home with his family after a three-day drive from his winter home in Alvin, Texas.

"My intentions are if they (Bavasi and Moss) don't reach an agreement by opening day then I plan on seeing the thing through. I really think their intentions are to wait until sometime after the All-Star break to see how I'm doing so they can make an offer."

Bavasi says he can understand Ryan's desire to settle his contract soon so he can concentrate on returning to the form that made him a 22-game winner in 1974.

"Unless I misunderstand him, Moss said we can talk at any time," said the general manager. "In August or September, if Ryan wants to talk about a new three-year contract we'll be happy to do so. But why would we do it now?

"He may be worth less money. He may be worth more money. It's a calculated risk on both our parts. I'm willing to take that risk."

Ryan's current contract is for $250,000 a year with a $200,000 bonus and $20,000 a year for five years after his retirement for a total of $1,050,000.

RYAN WAXES HOT...
SO DO POKER STAKES

by DICK MILLER   **JUNE 9, 1979**

ANAHEIM—Nolan Ryan is winning his poker game with Buzzie Bavasi.

It's a game the general manager of the Angels didn't want to join. His pitcher, after all, is an ace.

The stakes involved are at least $2 million in October and perhaps as high as $3 million when the free agent reentry draft rolls around again.

At 32 and in his final year of a three-year contract, The Express is again throwing like the man who shares the no-hitter record at four with Sandy Koufax, who can become baseball's all-time strikeout leader and who has won as many as 22 games with mediocre teams.

At the quarter pole of the season, The Express shut out Chicago for his fifth win against two losses, easily a 20-victory pace considering Ryan's habit of becoming more overpowering as the season progresses.

"Once, all I cared about were strikeouts," Ryan confessed in a rare moment of candor. "Now the pressure to shut off the opposition isn't like two or three years ago.

"We have a contending, explosive club. It gives you a lot of confidence without the constant pressure. You make your pitch and let the defense help you out."

The Bavasi-Ryan poker game has been going on for months and apparently won't end until the final game. Ryan and his agent, Dick Moss, began the game by giving Bavasi written permission to trade the pitcher to either Houston or the Texas Rangers at the winter baseball meetings, but to no other teams.

Bavasi tried to deal The Express to Texas along with Dave Chalk for outfielder Al Oliver, but was turned down. Then Bavasi turned down a deal with Houston for first baseman Bob Watson and reliever Joe Sambito (remember this was before Rod Carew came to Anaheim).

Moss and Ryan threw an idea into the pot and it wasn't a bluff: a four-year extension of the $1,050,000, three-year contract Ryan had negotiated himself with Harry Dalton.

"I don't blame him for trying, but I want to wait until after the All-Star Game to talk to him," Bavasi said at the time. "We're talking about a pitcher who was 10-13 last season and is 32 years old."

Through Moss, Ryan told Bavasi he would not negotiate during the season. If his contract wasn't extended prior to opening day, he was playing out his option.

It looked like a bad gamble for Ryan after his first start at Seattle. He was shelled for seven runs in 1 1/3 innings.

His accountant called Ryan the next day. "My computer says if you throw three consecutive full-game shutouts, your ERA will be back to under 3.00," said the accountant.

Ryan's ERA is 2.68. If you subtract first-inning bombings in Seattle and Boston, it drops to 0.87 for the seven other games.

The prospect of a six-month salary drive and the pot of gold awaiting at the end of the season has not eluded the gentlemanly Ryan.

"I'm a year older and a year wiser," he said with a grin as wide as a Texas prairie.

ANGELS CORRAL DOWNING, BUT RYAN EYES EXIT

by DICK MILLER　　　　　**NOVEMBER 3, 1979**

ANAHEIM—Now that catcher Brian Downing has signed a lucrative multi-year contract with the Angels, will Nolan Ryan and his agent, Dick Moss, alter their free-agent thinking—as Downing did—and come to terms with the California club?

Probably not, according to Moss.

Ryan, who has pitched for the Angels for eight seasons, appears more adamant than Downing in his desire to discover his value on the open market.

"It looks like I'll be a free agent after all," Ryan said after he and Moss met with general manager Buzzie Bavasi in Bavasi's Anaheim Stadium office shortly before Ryan departed for his Alvin, Texas, home.

Speculation that Downing might go the same route ended October 15 when the catcher signed with the Angels through 1983 for an estimated $1.8 million.

The Angels did make Ryan a written offer shortly after California was knocked out of the A.L. Championship Series by Baltimore. "I consider it equal to what (Montreal's) Bill Lee was offered," Moss said. "No disrespect to Bill, but Nolan is a little better pitcher than that."

Lee's contract is estimated at $1 million over three years.

"We'll select Nolan in the free-agent reentry draft and start negotiations from there," said Bavasi, sounding very much like a man who knew he had lost the senior Angel in point of service.

Bavasi denied that there was a personality conflict between himself and Moss, former counsel for the Major League Players Association, but did say he had turned the Ryan negotiations over to Mike Port, the Angels' player personnel director.

"Dick has his way of doing things and I have mine," was all the G.M. would say.

Bavasi will receive considerable heat if he allows Ryan to depart over a relatively small amount of dollars. The Angels have set attendance records in each of the last three years, there was an increased revenue from the playoff and the stadium is being enlarged to 70,000 for late in the 1980 season.

Ryan was the franchise through some awful years while Bavasi was in San Diego.

"Buzzie doesn't think what happened in the past counts," Ryan said, somewhat bitterly. "He says the only thing that counts is now.

"If I was healthy all season, I believe I would have won 20 games," The Express insisted.

And therein lies Bavasi's reluctance to offer Ryan a huge, long-term contract. He popped the elbow in his pitching arm at New York on July 25, shortly after missing an historic fifth no-hitter against the Yankees in Anaheim.

A few weeks later, Ryan popped a muscle in his right calf, one that he has pulled numerous times in the past.

"Mr. Bavasi," said Moss, "is on record as believing that pitchers should be paid less than other players, which is absurd.

"He also seems to believe that Nolan should accept less money because of his second half of the 1979 season, but I suspect that if the team hadn't been in contention, Nollie would have taken the proper time to heal and then been an effective pitcher for the last two weeks.

"Instead, he sacrificed, risked possible permanent injury, just so he could help win the title. I don't think he has ever received proper recognition for that."

Ryan had a 12-6 record with a 2.54 ERA at All-Star break, having 160 strikeouts at the time. He finished the year at 15-14 with a 3.60 ERA, and his seventh strikeout title (223).

GREEN ASTRO NOTES HALT THE EXPRESS

by KENNY HAND   **DECEMBER 1, 1979**

HOUSTON—Nolan Ryan always has been in the Houston Astros' backyard, but it took 12 years and a new ownership to make him part of the family.

The 33-year-old native of Alvin, Texas, a Houston suburb 26 miles down the road, signed a three-year contract worth $1 million a year on November 6. The contract, which provides for a fourth season in 1983 "at the option of the club," gives the Astros one of baseball's best starting staffs.

Ryan and James Rodney Richard led their respective leagues in strikeouts in 1979, Ryan carving his 223 total in his final year with the California Angels. Richard struck out 313, his second 300-plus strikeout season. In addition, the Astros can throw knuckleballer Joe Niekro, 21-11 last season, as part of any three-game series.

"Can you imagine this?" said Willie Stargell, the National League's co-MVP. "Hitting Niekro is like chasing a butterfly with the hiccups. Now they can sandwich him in there with Ryan and Richard. Man, for the first time the commissioner of baseball should tie up the deal for the next five years. By then, I'll be out of baseball."

The Astros, along with Texas, Milwaukee and the New York Yankees, were the leading teams in the free-agent scramble for Ryan, who has indicated for several years that he wanted to pitch for Houston or a team close to his home.

"Houston did everything in its power to sign me," said Ryan after coming to terms. "They pursued this thing very aggressively."

Ryan said his negotiating plan was to select one team and then listen to an offer, instead of becoming involved in a bidding war. It has been widely speculated that Ryan was considering only the two Texas teams and that Yankee owner George Steinbrenner would have to offer a gigantic amount to lure Ryan back to New York, where he once pitched for the Mets.

But it was the Astros and new owner John McMullen, a New York shipbuilder, who came through with the big money and McMullen has established a trend. Richard recently signed a four-year pact for $3.2 million and outfielder Jose Cruz was retained for $1.8 million over five years. "We want to keep our top players and make wise investments in the free-agent market," said McMullen, who bought Astrodomain for $19 million earlier this year.

"We feel Nolan Ryan is one of the best pitchers in the game. Can you see Nolan and J.R. in the same rotation with Niekro? We think we'll have a great pitching staff."

RANGERS FIRE $$ BLANKS AT RYAN

By Randy Galloway
December 1, 1979

ARLINGTON—The Texas Rangers not only didn't sign free agent Nolan Ryan, they never even made an offer.

And that just may say something about the so-called new image Brad Corbett is trying to project. The team's chairman of the board says he wants the finances and the thinking to be sound from now on.

In past years, it certainly wouldn't have made a difference to Corbett that the Rangers couldn't afford Ryan and actually had no business even drafting him.

He's the guy other baseball executives blame for escalating the free-agent market two years ago with that $2.8 million contract to Richie Zisk. At the time Zisk was signed, the Rangers were rolling in red ink.

"I don't want to point to specific contracts, but let's just say that on some of them I've learned my lesson the hard way," said Corbett, after announcing the Rangers were pulling out of the bidding for Ryan.

"Houston made a definite offer," said Corbett, "and I guess Nolan and Dick (Moss, Ryan's agent) would like us to do the same. But I wasn't going to make any blind offer like that.

"Moss said he wanted to make Nolan the highest-paid player in baseball," added Corbett, "but he's not going to do that at my expense.

"I'll say again that obviously we'd like to have Ryan, but it's obvious we're not going to get him. The money being talked about is more than we're willing to pay."

RYAN'S EXIT LEAVES ANGEL MEMORIES

by DICK MILLER   **DECEMBER 15, 1979**

ANAHEIM—There are scenes a reporter remembers most about Nolan Ryan, now with the Houston Astros, after eight years with the California Angels.

July 15, 1973, at Detroit. The Tigers' clownish first baseman, Norm Cash, was standing at the plate in the eighth inning when the plate umpire noticed he was swinging a piano leg instead of a baseball bat.

"Why not?" asked Cash. "I've got about as much chance with this as I have with a bat."

Of all Ryan's four no-hitters, this was the most awesome. He struck out 17 and walked four. The Express' arm stiffened after the Angels batted for 20 minutes and scored six times in the eighth inning; otherwise he probably would have struck out 21 to 23 batters.

September 27, 1977, at Anaheim Stadium. In the final inning of his last appearance of the season, The Express needed one strikeout to break Sandy Koufax's single-season record of 382.

In the 11th inning of his 41st game of the season, Ryan faced his final batter of the season, Minnesota's Rich Reese, and struck him out.

The Express made only three relief appearances as an Angel. Bobby Winkles, then managing, recalls an instance when he summoned Ryan out of the bullpen in the eighth inning of a 1974 game at the Big A.

A runner was in scoring position at second base for the White Sox and the dangerous Dick Allen at bat.

Both loved the challenge. Ryan walked off the mound and said, "Nothing but heat (fastballs), Dick." Allen nodded his head in agreement.

Ryan threw about 10 pitches, all in the 100-mph range. Allen, with one of the fastest bats ever, kept fouling them off to the right field side.

Finally, Allen flied to right field. A draw.

October 3, 1976. In the meeting at home plate prior to the last game of the season, A's manager Chuck Tanner told Angels' skipper Norm Sherry, "We are going to break the all-time record for stolen bases by a team in a season today."

Sherry smiled and relayed the word to Ryan.

The Express has a habit of checking the territory in front of the mound before making his first pitch. This day he also strolled to the third base foul line, peered into the Oakland dugout and said to Tanner, "I'll show you what you can do with your record."

The A's collected only two singles. Ryan struck out 14 and beat Mike Torrez, 1-0. No record.

August 20, 1974. The Angels were heading toward another sixth-place finish. Crowds and interest were dropping alarmingly and Dick Williams already had replaced Winkles as manager.

George Lederer, the Angels' late public relations director, came up with an idea that captured everyone's imagination: Time Ryan's famed express in actual game competition.

Ryan was battling Baltimore's Jim Palmer for a Cy Young Award and didn't need the added pressure. But he agreed to let Rockwell International scientists time him and the velocity to be posted on the scoreboard.

In a game against the Tigers, Ryan began by throwing in the 70 mph range. Not until the late innings did Ryan loosen up and reach the mid 90s. And then, in the late ninth inning, he set baseball's all-time record by throwing a ball 100.9 mph.

The bottom line on Ryan vs. Bavasi is this: Ryan kept interest in the club alive through some years when it would have had trouble beating the Pacific Coast League champion. That's worth something.

Bavasi refused to pay $3.56 million in guaranteed contracts to a pitcher he believes could break down in spring training.

So Ryan went to the Astros, 25 miles from his home. There is nothing wrong with either decision.

RYAN RAPS BAVASI...AGAIN

by DICK MILLER   **FEBRUARY 2, 1980**

ANAHEIM—Nolan Ryan, Dick Moss and Buzzie Bavasi have finally agreed on one subject after a year of debate.

They won't be exchanging Valentine's Day cards this month.

But the parties involved in Ryan's departure from the California Angels to the Houston Astros are still willing to throw daggers at each other at 30 paces.

Ryan returned to Orange County briefly and Moss, his agent, invited four baseball reporters to lunch with them. As the main course, Ryan and Moss launched new attacks on Bavasi, the Angels' general manager.

"My personal feelings are that the ballclub was not his No. 1 concern," said Ryan after noting published reports that Bavasi received 10 percent of the club's profits and therefore was reluctant to spend for talent.

"There were certain needs the ballclub had during the course of the season," the pitcher said. "I think if he'd spent a little money we would have improved ourselves with the people available and the time. There were a lot of ballplayers available June 15. Rudy May was available."

The Angels' senior player prior to his departure, Ryan also said there was a personal rift between Bavasi and manager Jim Fregosi.

"I think everybody was aware of the problem," said Ryan. "That problem has probably been here since some time shortly after Fregosi got here. I don't know what the problem is, but from the needs of the ballclub, the things that are said,

it's obvious.

"Personally, I think the only thing holding the Angels together is Jim Fregosi. If they don't get things settled, the club is going to be hurt."

Fregosi was away for a speaking engagement in Springfield, Illinois, and was unavailable for comment. "Jimmy and Buzzie did have some problems," said Mrs. Janet Fregosi, "but I think they are settled now."

Bavasi had little to add. "I'm not going to comment on anything," the veteran general manager said. "He's got his money, what does he want?"

Earlier, Bavasi had said there would be no problem in replacing Ryan, who had a 16-14 record in 1979. "All we need is two 8-and-7 pitchers," Bavasi said.

This little non-love affair has become a triangle involving Moss, a tough and talented attorney.

"I'm still angry," Moss said two months after the breakdown in negotiations. "Buzzie still thinks this is the mid-'50s and he is the general manager of the Dodgers and the name of the game is trying to sign a player for $15,000 when he's been authorized by Walter O'Malley to give him $16,000. All the talk about Buzzie getting a piece of the action, I don't think that is what it's about. He has to win. He has to beat people."

Said Bavasi:

"Those two young men (Moss and Ryan) deserve each other. We've had no trouble with any other agents."

RETURNING HOME

NOLAN RYAN

T he Ryan Express kept rolling as Ryan returned to Texas. Ryan played nine years for Houston and continued to add to his legend. In 1981, he claimed sole possession of the no-hitter record, throwing his fifth, against the Dodgers on September 26. He moved into first place on the career strikeouts list with K number 3,509 on April 27, 1983. His 40th birthday came and went, and he continued to throw the ball at speeds well upward of 90 miles per hour. Far from being ready for retirement, Ryan appeared to still be in his prime.

AP/Wide World Photos

TEXAS BOY COMES HOME

Can Nolan Ryan Put Astros into Orbit?

by DICK KAEGEL　　　　**APRIL 19, 1980**

ST. LOUIS—The Nolan Ryan file:

CLIP: "That Ryan," said umpire Durwood Merrill, "could throw the ball through a car wash without gettin' it wet."

PHOTO: Ryan's finger soaking in a jar of pickle brine to toughen it against blisters.

CLIP: Williams was still shaking in the clubhouse after being sent into the dirt by a high, inside fastball thrown by Nolan Ryan in the fourth inning..."Close to my head?" said No-Neck, incredulously. "It was right at it. There's only one thing I can think of at that point—death."

HEADLINES:

Ryan's No-No Spikes Royals' Protest

Ryan's Smoke Sends Tigers into No-Hit Blind

Ryan Roars into Feller's Class With 3rd Gem

Ryan's Pace: Four No-Hitters in Two-Year Span

PRESS RELEASE: The Angels have submitted Ryan's recent pitching speed record of 100.9 miles per hour to the *Guinness Book of World Records*.

CLIP: In the California clubhouse, he's addressed as Dr. Snake Oil, the healer who cured Clyde Wright's painful shoulder and his own aching right elbow. Ryan did it with oil from rattlesnakes. Honest!

CLIP: He is related through his mother to John Hancock, one of the signers of the Declaration of Independence.

HEADLINE: Nolan Ryan's Coverup: 1975 Was Living Hell

CLIP: "All I know," he says, "is that my next contract will be my last. I'll be 33 next year—old enough to realize you're starting to get pretty close to the finish."

PHOTO: Ryan, wide smile, holding a Houston Astros shirt.

The Sporting News file on Nolan Ryan, Jr., is thick and rich. It should be: Nolan Ryan has had a rich career and his record of pitching accomplishments is of epic proportion. His bank account is bulging as well.

He is the million-dollar-a-year man. After eight seasons of blowing his famous fastballs past American League batsmen on behalf of the California Angels, Ryan will throw his heat in the air-conditioned Astrodome and other National League parks.

The Astros are betting a $4 million free-agent investment that the righthander's presence will close the 1½-game gap that separated them from the West Division title last year.

> **Manager Bill Virdon, who must hide a sadistic bent behind that placid, spectacled countenance, plans to drop the fluttery knuckleball of Joe Niekro into his rotation right between the sizzling fastballs of J.R. Richard and Ryan.**

Manager Bill Virdon, who must hide a sadistic bent behind that placid, spectacled countenance, plans to drop the fluttery knuckleball of Joe Niekro into his rotation right between the sizzling fastballs of J.R. Richard and Ryan.

"That's a nice variety for someone in the stands," catcher Alan Ashby said dryly, "but for the catcher, I don't know. But I'd rather be the catcher than a batter. I don't think any ballclub in the league is going to be anxious to see Houston come to town."

Last season Richard struck out 313, an N.L. record for a righthander, after getting 303 the previous year. Ryan broke Sandy Koufax's one-season record with 383 strikeouts in 1973 and has gone over 300 five times. He entered this season just 91 strikeouts shy of 3,000 for his career. Only three pitchers—Walter Johnson (3,508), Gaylord Perry (3,141) and Bob Gibson (3,117)—have more.

With such strikeout power available, the Astros have punched up all manner of statistics. The figures show, for example, that Ryan has averaged 9.78 strikeouts per nine innings—better than Koufax's 9.27 average for Los Angeles. (Richard's average for his relatively brief career is 8.92 strikeouts per nine innings, a bright future as well.)

It was in 1971 that the New York Mets, de-

lighted with Ryan's fastball but despairing of his wildness, dispatched him to California in a deal that netted them infielder Jim Fregosi (who wound up as Nolan's last manager with the Angels). In the A.L., Ryan bloomed into a strikeout star who twice was a 20-game winner and compiled a 138-121 record despite being with a second-division club in six of eight seasons.

There was a scare in 1975 when numbing elbow pain kept him from combing his hair or brushing his teeth. Stubbornly, he kept the ailment to himself and kept pitching but underwent surgery for the bone chips after that season. His career survived.

Ryan lets out a yawn as he sits in the dugout watching a game between the Astros and the Dodgers in Los Angeles.

If Houston fans wondered why the Astros would pay a million a year to a guy who was 16-14 in the Angels' division-winning season of '79, they should note Ryan was 12-6 at the All-Star break and then was hampered by an elbow injury and a pulled calf muscle.

"Everything's fine now," he said.

And Texas undoubtedly cringed when Ryan's spring training outings were disasters. His spring stats: Three games, 12 innings, 23 hits, 17 runs, five walks, nine strikeouts.

But Ryan patiently explained he is traditionally a slow starter.

"If I ever had to make a club on the basis of my spring training performances, I'd never succeed," he said.

Aside from his on-the-mound flair for smoke and fury, Ryan has given a measure of color to baseball. The New York press loved it when they discovered Ryan toughened his fingers against blisters by soaking them in pickle brine. And the California press loved it when they discovered he was dispensing a snake oil rub in the Angels' clubhouse. He has his moments of pique—he once publicly questioned fellow pitcher Frank Tanana's dedication and he feuded with Billy Martin over his All-Star snub in 1977.

But Ryan remains your basic small-town boy from Alvin, Texas, near Houston. He lives on a ranch and runs some cattle and is quite content sloshing about in mud and manure.

Ryan grew up in Alvin, youngest of six children. His late father worked for an oil company; his mother still lives in the home from whence young Nolan ventured forth to deliver newspapers.

Ryan and daughter Wendy, 4, take care of chores at home in Alvin, Texas.

AP/Wide World Photos

"People always knew when I was delivering," Ryan said with a wry smile, "because I always put them right on the front porch, right next to the door. I had pinpoint control in those days."

Ryan was talking one spring day in Cocoa, Florida, basking in the sun with wife Ruth, his childhood sweetheart, by his side. Reese, 4, and Wendy, 3, clambered on and off his lap.

Ryan said, no, he didn't think he'd lost any velocity. And, no, the millions the Astros are pressing into his hands hadn't changed him. ("Oh, it enables you to do more, but it hasn't changed me.")

And, no, folks back in Alvin don't make much of a fuss over him.

"They treat me like any normal citizen and that's the way I want to be," he said. "I've never liked the attention or notoriety of major league baseball."

Even in Alvin, though, kids are kids. One day, son Reid, 8, forgot his lunch money. Nolan took the change to school but before he left the classroom, a boy jumped up and declared, "That's not Reid's father, that's Nolan Ryan, the baseball player!" An instant autograph session unfolded and, wife Ruth said later, it embarrassed the pitcher.

How's he been treated in the Astros' clubhouse—any resentment because of his rich contract?

"Naw, I haven't noticed any," he said. "I think baseball players are starting to accept that this is a way of life in the game. People in the game are realizing that when you go with free agency, there are risks involved and there can be a certain amount of reward at the end too."

And the fans?

"I know some of them will hold my contract against me," he said. "I just hope they don't expect me to be 20-2. I've never been a 20-2 pitcher and I can't expect that even of myself. I hope the fans will appreciate that I try to pitch the best Nolan Ryan can pitch."

When Ryan first unleashed his arm this spring in batting practice, he whistled a pitch a bit too close to Craig Reynolds. "Mr. Ryan, sir," said Reynolds, in a parody of the Mean Joe Greene television commercial, "would you like part of my Coke?"

Replied Mean Nolan: "If it's all the same to you, I'd rather have part of your ribs."

That's something the Astros hope National League batters keep in the back of their minds.

AP/Wide World Photos

NOLAN
From
Alvin to **R**YAN
Cooperstown

Ryan beats the runner to first base.

The day after his sixth no-hitter, Ryan continued his training regimen while his teammates took batting practice.

AP/Wide World Photos

AP/Wide World Photos

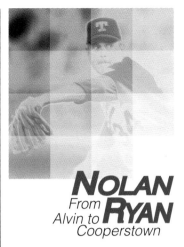

NOLAN RYAN
From Alvin to Cooperstown

In his 27 major league seasons, Ryan compiled a win-loss record of 324-292.

Ryan fires one home during his 300th victory, July 31, 1990, at County Stadium in Milwaukee.

NOLAN *RYAN*
From Alvin to Cooperstown

Ryan and his oldest son, Reid, talk to the media after facing each other in a 1991 exhibition pitching duel.

AP/Wide World Photos

Ryan is carried off the field by teammates after pitching his seventh no-hitter, this one against the Toronto Blue Jays on May 1,1991.

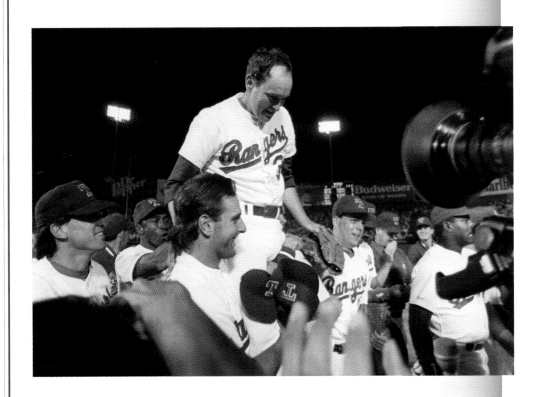

Louis DeLuca

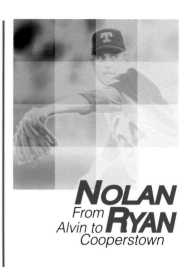

NOLAN RYAN
From Alvin to Cooperstown

Ryan, with his wife, Ruth, waves to the crowd in Anaheim after his #30 jersey was retired during his induction into the Angels' Hall of Fame in 1992.

Hall-of-Famers Ryan and George Brett pose for photographers on October 3,1993, just before their retirement.

NOLAN RYAN
From Alvin to Cooperstown

Ryan's strict fitness regimen was one of the keys to his longevity. Here, he stretches during a workout at the Rangers' spring training facility.

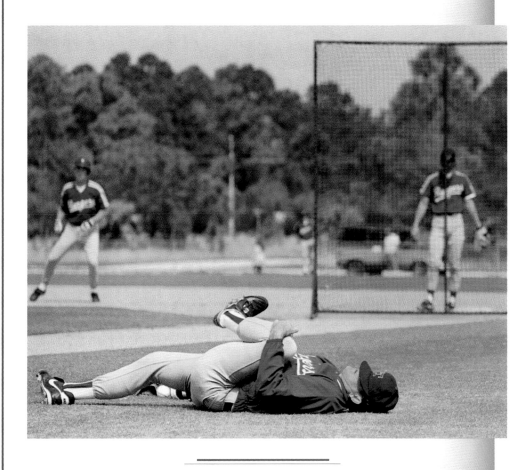

Louis DeLuca

As a member of the Texas Rangers' staff, Ryan led the American League in strikeouts in 1989 and in 1990.

Louis DeLuca

NOLAN RYAN

From Alvin to Cooperstown

Ryan tried to accommodate as many autograph seekers as possible.

NOLAN RYAN
From Alvin to Cooperstown

Ryan, Ruth, Reid, Reese, and Wendy (left to right) during Nolan Ryan Day ceremonies in Arlington.

The Sporting News

Ryan receives a standing ovation from the home crowd on Nolan Ryan Day.

The Sporting News

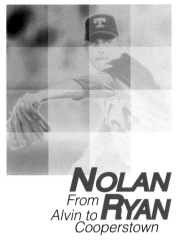

NOLAN RYAN
From
Alvin to
Cooperstown

With seven no-hitters, 5,714 strikeouts, and a 90+ mph fastball, Hall-of-Famer Ryan was one of the most intimidating pitchers in baseball.

Louis DeLuca

ASTROS FIND BATTING EYES AS HURLING SAGS

by HARRY SHATTUCK

JULY 19, 1980

HOUSTON—Just when it seemed the Houston pitching staff had become invincible, James Rodney Richard had a problem with his arm, Nolan Ryan a problem with an umpire and the other hurlers a problem with opposing batters.

Wonder of wonders, though, the Astros discovered they possess an offense, too, and suddenly the Astrodome was the scene of games with scores of 8-5, 9-2, 5-4 and—gulp!—even 12-10.

"I believe J.R. is fine," manager Bill Virdon said, "but you have to be concerned about any pitcher who has arm soreness. He's thrown a lot of baseballs the past five years (at least 200 innings each season and more than 290 innings twice)."

Ryan, the other half of the awesome twosome, was maintaining one of the league's best ERAs (2.88), but had only a 5-5 record. His up-and-down season reached a low on June 29 in a 12-10 triumph over the Reds, in which Ryan and his teammates disagreed fre-

AP/Wide World Photos

quently with umpire Lanny Harris.

"I've seen Ryan before and he tries to show up the umpires by asking about ball and strike calls," said Harris, the home plate arbiter. "I made up my mind I wasn't going to put up with it."

Catcher Luis Pujols said Harris told him he'd watched Ryan on television and didn't like what he saw.

Ryan watched Harris from 60 feet, 6 inches and didn't like what he saw. He felt he was squeezed "by the smallest strike zone I've ever had to pitch to." Virdon called Harris' strike zone "terrible" and let the umpire know it in such a way as to earn the Astros' first ejection of the season.

Astronotes: Ryan recorded his 3,000th career strikeout when he fanned Cesar Geronimo for the third of six whiffs on July 4 in an 8-1 loss to the Reds. Walter Johnson, Gaylord Perry and Bob Gibson were the first three to fan 3,000 batters. Ironically, Geronimo also was Gibson's 3,000th victim.

RYAN AND RICHARD HEADED LOW-HIT LIST

by CARL CLARK **1981**

Although run production in the big leagues fell almost four percent from its 1979 level, major league pitchers were able to limit the opposition to two or fewer hits only 50 times in 1980, the lowest total since the 32 of 1962.

The American League, despite the lack of a hitless game for the third consecutive season, had more low-hit games than the National, which had a no-hitter by Los Angeles' Jerry Reuss. There were eight one-hit games in the A.L., five fewer than the record number spun in '79, and 21 two-hitters. The National League had only four one-hitters and 16 two-hitters. In '79, there were 10 one-hitters in the N.L. and 24 two-hitters.

The Astros, who had the lowest ERA in the majors, led the way in low-hit games. They turned in five, and bullet-throwing righthanders J.R. Richard and Nolan Ryan, with a little help from Joe Sambito, accounted for all of them.

Ryan had the majors' greatest involvement in low-hitters, with a pair of two-hitters and a one-hitter that he shared with Sambito.

In none of those games, however, did Ryan go into the late innings with a chance for a record fifth no-hitter. Garry Templeton broke up his June 19 one-hitter against St. Louis with a third-inning blooper that fell on the left-field line for a double. His first two-hitter, May 28 against San Diego, also was marked by a third-inning double, this time by pitcher Rick Wise. Ozzie Smith added an infield single in the eighth. The Cubs' only hits off Ryan on August 24 were a triple by Larry Biittner in the fifth and an eighth-inning single by Tim Blackwell.

AP/Wide World Photos

COOLEST IN DOME? NO-HIT RYAN

by HARRY SHATTUCK   **OCTOBER 10, 1981**

HOUSTON—With every pitch, with every out carrying Nolan Ryan toward baseball history, the tension became more unbearable for his Houston teammates who care so much about this good ol' country boy turned big city hero.

"I was so nervous I squeezed the cover off the baseball I was holding in our dugout," said fellow Astros pitcher Joe Niekro.

"I've watched some great achievements during my career but I've never felt so emotionally drained over a game," said pitcher Don Sutton.

"I was standing at shortstop thinking, 'Move this way a step; no, move the other way; whatever you do, don't mess up this one,'" said shortstop Craig Reynolds.

Only one Astro remained completely unflappable. "Shoot, I don't get emotional about these things anymore," Ryan would say after becoming the first major leaguer ever to pitch five no-hitters.

"This is something I've wanted to accomplish for a long time. But I've been there too many times before in the late innings. I was beginning to think I didn't have the stamina to get the fifth one."

On September 26, the marvelous Mr. Ryan had the stamina, the heart and the talent to shut down a Los Angeles offense rated among the best in the National League. Ryan walked three and struck out 11. The Astros gave him enough support for a 5-0 victory. The performance lowered Ryan's league-leading ERA to 1.74.

Ryan, 34, pitched four no-hitters in the mid-1970s with the California Angels. Now he has surpassed the record he shared with Dodgers Hall of Famer Sandy Koufax. Ryan also has thrown seven one-hitters.

He labeled this his favorite no-hitter. And not primarily because the game was televised nationally by NBC. Rather, it was because his wife, Ruth, his mother and other family members and close friends were in the Astrodome rooting. Later they were on the AstroTurf hugging Nolan and crying tears of joy.

"And because this is the first no-hitter I've pitched during a pennant race late in the season," Ryan added.

When Ryan came home two winters ago to sign with the Astros as a free agent, skeptics forecast imminent discord in the Astros' clubhouse. He had signed what at the time was the richest contract in baseball history. He would make $1.125 million per season. Surely his teammates would be jealous.

He was joining an organization starving for national attention and his picture—Nolan Ryan's picture, not a veteran Astro's picture—was on the cover of dozens of magazines. Surely his teammates would be envious.

"It's impossible not to like Nolan," right fielder Terry Puhl said, once the euphoria of the no-hit celebration had died and the last champagne cork had popped. "Here is a guy who makes so much money, yet his style of living and his concern for his family are as genuine as with any person I've ever met. He is a man with class."

"He fit in from the moment he joined this club," Niekro said. "For all the pressure, all the strain he went through last year (as a million-dollar athlete performing in his back yard), he never stopped being Nolan the team man, a guy we all rooted for and cared about."

"He'd fit in any place he went," pitcher Joe Sambito said. "Any team, any business. He's his own person. He goes about his business in a private way. At the park, he kids with us and is simply one of the guys. But when he's got the ball and takes the mound, you can see him change. He has that look about him that says, 'Nobody is going to beat me.' He is such a gamer."

Ryan was indeed a gamer this day. He struggled early, throwing 65 pitches the first three innings, 81 pitches through the fourth. He walked three Dodgers. He was continuously behind on the count.

"He said after the third inning that his delivery was messed up, his back was killing him and that he just didn't feel right," Astros pitcher Dave Smith remembered. "Well, mess up my delivery, kill my back and tell me not to feel right."

Nolan retired the last 19 Dodger batters. "I let up a little bit in the late innings," Ryan said. "I didn't get as many strikeouts (10 in the first six innings, only one in the final three) but I had better control."

He certainly didn't let up in the ninth. He threw three straight strikes past leadoff pinch-hitter Reggie Smith, the third a 97-mph fastball. He coaxed an easy grounder from Ken Landreaux.

But the last obstacle offered the toughest of challenges. Dusty Baker, batting .322 and a superb clutch hitter, strode to the plate. And if Ryan pitched around Baker, ever-dangerous Steve Garvey was on deck.

"I wasn't nervous," Baker said. "I was thinking that I didn't know of anybody else I'd rather have at the plate in that situation than me."

"I was hoping to get a chance," Garvey said. "You envision a situation that two men are out in the ninth and you're the batter who breaks up the no-hitter. I wanted that chance."

But it was only a vision. Baker worked a 2-0 count, then Ryan threw a curve—his out pitch most of the day—and Baker grounded feebly to third base to touch off a mob scene at the mound.

"Superman couldn't have hit him today once he started getting his breaking ball over," said Astros center fielder Tony Scott.

"A team of Supermen couldn't have hit him," said Houston pitcher J. R. Richard, who understands Superman-type mound work.

Ryan needed one superb defensive play, a running catch by Puhl near the right-center field wall to rob Mike Scioscia of extra bases in the seventh inning.

Said Astros catcher Alan Ashby, whose boyhood idol was Koufax, "As long as I live, I'll never forget being a part of Nolan Ryan's fifth no-hitter."

September 26, 1981
Houston 5, Los Angeles 0

LOS ANGELES	ab	r	h	bi	HOUSTON	ab	r	h	bi
Lopes 2b	3	0	0	0	Puhl rf	4	1	1	0
Smith ph	1	0	0	0	Garner 2b	4	0	2	1
Landreaux cf	3	0	0	0	T. Scott cf	5	1	0	0
Baker lf	4	0	0	0	Cruz lf	4	1	3	1
Garvey 1b	2	0	0	0	Ashby c	4	0	1	2
Guerrero 3b	3	0	0	0	Howe 3b	4	0	0	0
Scioscia c	3	0	0	0	Spilman 1b	2	0	0	0
Roenicke rf	3	0	0	0	Pittman ph	1	0	1	0
Thomas ss	2	0	0	0	Walling 1b	0	1	0	0
Power p	1	0	0	0	Reynolds ss	4	1	2	1
Perconte ph	1	0	0	0	RYAN p	2	0	1	0
Goltz p	0	0	0	0					
Forster p	0	0	0	0					
Johnstone ph	1	0	0	0					
TOTALS	27	0	0	0		32	5	11	5

```
Los Angeles   0 0 0   0 0 0   0 0 0—0
Houston       0 0 2   0 0 0   0 3 x—5
```

E—Thomas. LOB—Los Angeles 3, Houston 12. 2B—Cruz, Reynolds. 3B—Reynolds. SB—Garner, Garvey, Thomas, Cruz. S—Ryan.

LOS ANGELES	IP	H	R	ER	BB	SO
Power (L 1-3)	3⅓	6	2	1	3	1
Goltz	⅔	0	0	0	0	0
Forster	3	2	0	0	1	2
Stewart	⅓	2	3	3	2	0
Howe	⅔	1	0	0	0	0

HOUSTON						
Ryan (W 10-5)	9	0	0	0	3	11

Ashby may have put Ryan's reaction and the Astros' respect for him in perspective when he said:

"He has just completed one of the great accomplishments in baseball history. And how will he celebrate? He'll hop in his truck, drive to the ranch and be with his family. He's just a country boy working in the big city. And a real good person."

Not a bad pitcher, either.

RYAN'S FIVE GEMS

Following are Nolan Ryan's five no-hit performances, four of which he pitched for the California Angels before his record fifth with the Houston Astros. (H) denotes home games, (A) away games.

DATE	OPPONENT	SCORE
May 15, 1973	Kansas City (A)	3-0
July 15, 1973	Detroit (A)	6-0
Sept. 28, 1974	Minnesota (H)	4-0
June 1, 1975	Baltimore (H)	1-0
Sept. 26, 1981	Los Angeles (H)	5-0

Ryan delivers a pitch during his record-setting fifth no-hitter.

RYAN EXPRESS BACK ON TRACK

July 1982

HOUSTON—Nolan Ryan's season was only eight games old when the skeptics began whispering.

Had the Ryan Express lost his hummer? The Houston Astros righthander had a 2-6 record. His earned-run average was above 5.00. He already had permitted more runs in eight starts than in all 21 starts last season.

Some people close to the Astros even began to wonder if the club would exercise its option to employ Ryan next year in the fourth and final season of his contract, which calls for $1.125 million per year.

Ryan has answered his critics. The fastball isn't gone. The strikeouts continue. Indeed, Ryan is fanning batters at a better rate than last season, when he was the National League ERA champion.

Ryan recently extended his major league record to 142 games in which he has struck out 10 or more batters. He fanned 10 or more four straight times in late June and early July. In the process, he squared his record at 9-9.

"I've just been in a good groove," Ryan said. "My fastball has been effective. So has my curve. And I've been throwing more change ups than in other years."

Ryan had moved within 30 strikeouts of Gaylord Perry, who ranks second on baseball's all-time strikeout list and still is active. At his current pace, Ryan could surpass career leader Walter Johnson's total of 3,508 strikeouts next year.

Ryan felt he was throwing well even at the start of the season when he wasn't winning. "One bad inning each game was hurting me," he said. "I felt as good as I ever did."

Probably his most impressive performance of the year came July 16 against Pittsburgh in the Astrodome. He struck out 10 and dominated the hot-hitting Pirates all night, but it was his finish that left even his teammates in disbelief. Ryan's last four pitches, Nos. 123 through 126 for the game, were clocked at 94 mph. "He broke the webbing of my glove on a third strike to Dave Parker," catcher Luis Pujols said.

Houston starters completed nine of 12 games during one stretch, and in that period no starter went less than seven innings.

That was solving the Astros' bullpen problem, but not necessarily the club's losing problem. Ryan, Don Sutton, Bob Knepper and Joe Niekro all lost low-scoring heartbreakers.

"I'm seeing a lot of dreams slip away," Sutton said. "I wish I could see a light at the end of the tunnel. But I can't."

"I don't foresee things getting much better," Ryan said. "I see a long year for us."

NOLAN RYAN: A STRIKING PERFORMER

by HARRY SHATTUCK   **MAY 9, 1983**

HOUSTON—His critics have been numerous and outspoken.

He isn't consistent, they said. He is too wild, too concerned about strikeouts and is barely a .500 pitcher, so they said.

No matter that the teams for which he has toiled—the New York Mets, California Angels and Houston Astros—usually have compiled far worse records than Nolan Ryan. No matter that since 1968, his first full year in the major leagues, Ryan has been among the most durable pitchers in the game, averaging 30 starts per year, never starting fewer than 21 games. No matter that, on any given day, he is the most dominant pitcher of his era, the author of a record five no-hitters.

The critics shake their heads and say his career record is "only" 207-187, and that this man is not a giant of his sport.

That's one reason, perhaps the main reason, why the pursuit of Walter Johnson's career strikeout record has been so important to Nolan Ryan, why a normally soft-spoken, even reticent

Ryan waves to an appreciative crowd in Houston.

man has warmed to the acclaim he has received this year.

"I think this will draw some attention and respect to me that hasn't been there before," Ryan says. "My critics, some of whom can't find too much positive to say about my career, will have to take notice of this.

"A lot of people say I'm just a .500 pitcher or that I walk too many batters. In a way, it's kind of funny that I'm getting the attention now for strikeouts. Earlier in my career, people said that was my problem, that I tried to strike out too many hitters.

"But I think it (breaking the record) will make people take notice after they study the record. They'll see that I did in 16 years what took Johnson 21 years, that I've been durable, pitched a lot of innings and I have been consistent."

Ryan broke Johnson's 55-year-old record April 27, recording career strikeout No. 3,509 when he threw a called third strike past Montreal pinch-hitter Brad Mills in the eighth inning of a 4-2 Houston victory at Olympic Stadium.

The irony is that, while Ryan now is gaining plaudits for his strikeouts, he has in recent years developed into something beyond a pure strikeout pitcher.

Yes, he remains capable of high strikeout totals. He fanned 10 or more batters 10 times last year, improving his major league record to 145 games of double-figure strikeouts. But the 17- and 18-strikeout games apparently are in the past, traded in for better command and control.

"I think I came to the majors with the disease of all power pitchers," Ryan says. "When I got in trouble, I'd reach back and try to overthrow. Getting away from that is nothing that came overnight. It came a little bit in my first years with the Angels (the early 1970s). I think it comes with maturity."

During his three-plus seasons with Houston, Ryan has said periodically, "I don't strike out as

Ryan, who has a career batting average of .110, prepares to lay down a bunt.

many batters, but I think I'm a better pitcher." His performance says he is right.

In 1981, his 1.69 earned-run average was the best in the National League, indeed the best ERA in the N.L. since Bob Gibson's 1.12 in 1968.

In 1982, during one stretch he was 9-1; in July, in 54²/₃ innings, his ERA was 1.10.

Since he joined the Astros, his strikeout-walk ratio is about 2¹/₂-to-1, a far cry from 1974 and 1977 when, as an Angel, he walked more than 200 batters both seasons.

He remains very, very difficult to hit. Late in the 1981 season, he produced his fifth no-hitter. Last season, he pitched his eighth one-hitter and 18th two-hitter. Overall, in those two years, he permitted only 295 hits in 399¹/₃ innings, a remarkable ratio, considering his age.

Nolan Ryan is 36 now, an age when fastball pitchers are supposed to be retired, perhaps scouting or selling insurance or raising cattle.

Ryan raises cattle, but only in his spare time.

He lives in a ranch-style home in Alvin, about 20 miles south of Houston, where Nolan grew up and married his high school sweetheart, Ruth. His $1 million-per-year contract has brought Ryan riches, but his tastes remain simple. Down-home, as Texans say. Given a choice of traveling the world or working outside at home, he prefers the latter. He can afford caviar, but he'd prefer chicken-fried steak. He is Alvin's favorite son, and proud of it.

As an athlete, he is the same. Never a phony, never one to flaunt his ability or his talent, never one to solicit publicity, Nolan Ryan nevertheless enjoys above all throwing a baseball. Hard. And he knows that when the day comes that he can't throw hard, he will walk away from the game.

"I don't anticipate being around another four or five years," Ryan says with typical candor. "I won't change the kind of pitcher I am just to stay around. You live by the sword, you die by the sword.

"I'm not going to develop a knuckleball or call (former teammate) Don Sutton and ask him how he scuffs a ball. The style of pitcher I am, I can't see me going any longer than the day I lose it."

Ryan can see himself lasting another two or three years, though. He'd like to see himself lasting through that period as an Astro. But the contract he signed in November 1979, the richest pact ever awarded a pitcher at the time, expires after this season. And Ryan's future is not at all certain.

During the winter both Ryan and club management seemed to agree that a contract extension was in order. But the Astros suggested Ryan take less pay this year than his original contract specified in return for guarantees in 1984 and 1985. Ryan deemed that a pay cut. "I see no reason they should expect me to take a pay cut on a contract I signed four years ago," the pitcher said.

General manager Al Rosen has said he prefers not to negotiate contracts during the season, that he fully expects to sign Ryan once this year is over. "I want Nolan to remain with our club because he's not only a good pitcher but he's also a good person," Rosen says.

Ryan, who joined the Astros through free agency, is ineligible to participate in the re-entry draft again until the fall of 1984. So his options this winter, if no agreement is reached, are to retire, request a trade or take the club to arbitration, the most likely alternative.

Based on the early season, the Astros can ill afford to lose Ryan. Their home attendance after 15 home games was about 150,000 behind last year's pace. They were averaging about 12,000 per home date until Ryan made his first bid (unsuccessful) to break the strikeout record against Montreal in the Astrodome (April 22) and drew 32,000.

Beyond that, the Astros no longer are the pitching-rich club they were earlier in this decade. Simply stated, they need Nolan Ryan not only as a gate attraction but as a continuing winner.

"Durability has been the one thing about my career that has surprised a lot of people," Ryan says. "I know some people have expected me to lose it for quite a few years. Most power pitchers start to lose it around 32 or so. But I still have good leg strength. Physically, I feel as good as I did when I came over here."

"In addition to his great talent, the only way he could have set this kind of record is because of his great endurance," said Montreal manager Bill Virdon, Ryan's manager the previous three years at Houston. "It's almost a superhuman accomplishment. It's an exceptional feat just to stay physically strong for such a long period. Nolan has had a phenomenal career."

"This is one tremendous feat," said Expos first baseman Al Oliver, the defending National League batting champion. "It shows consistency and longevity. These are exactly the same kind of ingredients that should automatically put a player into the Hall of Fame."

Since joining the Astros, two goals have been cited frequently by Ryan. One is team-oriented, to pitch Houston into the World Series. And anyone who doubts his sincerity would have been touched seeing him in tears fully an hour after the most painful defeat in Astros history—the loss to Philadelphia in the fifth and deciding game of the 1980 National League Championship Series.

The other goal was personal: Johnson's strikeout record, the record many baseball loyalists said would never be broken. Ryan fully expects Philadelphia's Steve Carlton to pass him, perhaps this year. "But it's important for me to be first," he said.

Ryan wanted to establish the record before his home fans, his family, his friends. And April 22, needing to whiff eight Phillies, he had that chance. "But I could tell warming up in the bullpen I wasn't strong," Ryan said. "My velocity was good (98 mph, a speed any rookie flame-thrower would relish), but my curve was missing. It was very disappointing."

It was also a mere matter of time. Ryan had said he hoped to set the record by striking out Pete Rose, and he meant that as a compliment just as Rose had intended his remark two years ago that he'd be honored to set the National League hit record against Ryan (he tied the mark against the Astros pitcher). Against the Expos on April 27, Ryan was less selective. "I'll settle for striking out a pitcher," he said.

When his pursuit of the record was over, Ryan said he felt "relief more than excitement. I never get too excited about anything."

Baseball officials didn't get excited. Commissioner Bowie Kuhn was notably absent in Montreal. So was National League president Chub Feeney. So were Astros owner John McMullen and Rosen.

It was left for Virdon to say, "This ranks on a par with Hank Aaron breaking Babe Ruth's home run record."

Ryan rates this accomplishment only third among the 26 records he shares or holds, behind his fifth no-hitter for Houston against Los Angeles in 1981 and his 383 strikeouts for California in 1973.

He was pressed for comparisons with others but said, "I don't compare myself to anyone, not to Sandy Koufax or Walter Johnson or Bob Feller or any strikeout pitcher."

But the comparisons with Johnson are inevitable. Both were gracious gentlemen. Both emphasized conditioning. Both avoided smoking and heavy drinking. Both were durable. And both threw blazing fastballs.

The former strikeout king once pitched three shutouts in four days for Washington, a five-hitter on Friday, a three-hitter Saturday and a two-hitter Monday, missing Sunday only because of blue laws.

Walter Johnson thrived for 21 seasons and compiled an amazing 2.37 earned-run average.

The new strikeout king recalls his first major league game September 11, 1966, with the Mets. "I was pitching against the Braves. I was 19 years old and I was scared to death," Ryan says. "I had all the baseball cards of Henry Aaron and Eddie Mathews and the other great Braves hitters. And I wondered what in the world I was doing out there."

His first strikeout victim wasn't Aaron. It was opposing pitcher Pat Jarvis. Regardless, a record-shattering career was born. And some spring or summer day, years from now, perhaps when another frightened 19-year-old is beginning an illustrious career, historians will still refer to Walter Johnson, The Big Train, baseball legend. But they will also point to Nolan Ryan, The Express, baseball legend.

AP/Wide World Photos

Ryan, covering home against the Padres, finished his career with only 90 errors.

RYAN DOESN'T APPEAR TO BE SLOWING DOWN

July 29, 1985

HOUSTON—In a week that was memorable even for Nolan Ryan, the Houston Astros' pitcher on July 11 became the first man in baseball history to record 4,000 career strikeouts. Five days later, Ryan pitched three shutout innings in the All-Star Game, by far his best showing as an All-Star.

Ryan struck out Danny Heep of the New York Mets on three pitches for strikeout No. 4,000. In seven innings against the Mets, Ryan struck out 11 and raised his career total to 4,004.

As was the case when he pitched his record-setting fifth no-hitter in 1981 and when he broke Walter Johnson's strikeout record of 3,508 in 1983, Ryan seemed happy to get his 4,000th strikeout out of the way.

"This ranks up there with breaking Walter Johnson's record, but I'm not much of a goal-setter where numbers are concerned," said Ryan. "My goal when I came here was to pitch in the World Series as an Astro, and it still is."

At Minneapolis, he worked the middle three innings of the All-Star Game, allowing two hits and no runs while striking out two. In three previous All-Star Games, Ryan had allowed seven hits and five runs in five innings.

"I guess you could call this a vintage Nolan Ryan performance—a few walks, a few strikeouts," said Ryan, who also walked two batters. "They say some things never change."

Ryan's ability to strike out hitters despite his age is one of them. Ryan, 38, once again is among the National League leaders and remains one of the most feared pitchers in baseball.

One goal Ryan does talk about is his desire to pitch 20 years in the major leagues. He is in his 18th season and shows no signs of weakening.

"I've signed a contract through 1987 that will enable me to get 20 years," he said. "All I have to do is stay healthy."

If Ryan pitches through '87, he could finish his career with nearly 4,500 strikeouts. It's possible that record would go down with Cy Young's 511 wins and Joe DiMaggio's 56-game hitting streak as unbreakable.

"It's a record that will stand for 15 or more years," said Ryan. "Dwight Gooden (of the Mets) has to be considered. But if it's done, it'll probably be in the American League. Pitchers pitch more innings because of the designated hitter. That's the thing about the National League. A pitcher who pitches for a team that doesn't score many runs is going to have trouble getting the innings in."

Ryan has pitched in both leagues, spending eight years with the California Angels. Since coming to Houston in 1980, Ryan's durability hasn't diminished.

In addition, criticism that Ryan is merely a .500 pitcher who goes for strikeouts has been quieted. In five-plus seasons with the Astros, his record is 72-53. Overall, Ryan's record is 239-212. Should Ryan pitch successfully for two more seasons, he could finish with about 275 career wins.

"He stays in such great shape," said manager Bob Lillis. "He'll pitch as long as he wants to. His accomplishments are a combination of everything—desire, ability, durability and his competitiveness."

Two A.L. hitters learned about Ryan's competitive nature during the All-Star Game. High and tight pitches from Ryan sent Rickey Henderson and Dave Winfield of the New York Yankees sprawling.

"I'm not out there to hurt anyone, but for me to be the best pitcher I can be, I have to be aggressive," Ryan said. "I'm a power pitcher. That's the way I've pitched my entire career. I'm not the nicest guy in the world when I walk on the field."

Ryan tips his hat to the crowd after striking out Danny Heep of the New York Mets for the 4,000th K of his career.

THE LEGEND GROWS

NOLAN RYAN

I n December 1988, Texas Rangers fans received an early Christmas present—the team announced that Nolan Ryan was coming to town. After nine seasons in Houston, the 41-year-old Ryan joined the Rangers with five no-hitters and 4,775 career strikeouts. He also remained in possession of a blistering fastball. On August 22, 1989, Rickey Henderson swung and missed to become the 5,000th victim of the Ryan Express. But Ryan wasn't done. He pitched his sixth no-hitter on June 11, 1990, and added a seventh (and final) no-hit game on May 8, 1991. Unfortunately, all good things must come to an end, and in February 1993, Ryan announced that the upcoming season would be his last.

AP/Wide World Photos

TEXAS-SIZE DEALS BY RANGERS

by PHIL ROGERS   **DECEMBER 19, 1988**

ATLANTA—Tom Grieve called it "one of the greatest days" in the history of the Texas Rangers when he signed Nolan Ryan to a $2 million contract December 7.

Landing the free agent pitcher who has pitched five no-hitters and is baseball's career strikeout leader, with a total of 4,775, put the finishing touch on Grieve's overhaul of the Rangers. The general manager took center stage at the winter meetings by pulling off five transactions involving 17 players in the span of three days.

Grieve's attempt to rebuild an offense that dropped from 5.1 runs a game in 1987 to an average of 4.0 last year brought the Rangers .300 hitters Rafael Palmeiro from the Chicago Cubs and Julio Franco from the Cleveland Indians. In return, Grieve traded away Mitch Williams, a potentially dominating left-handed stopper, and three members of

Ryan fields questions from the media after signing with the Texas Rangers.

Texas' 1988 opening-day lineup—first baseman Pete O'Brien, center fielder Oddibe McDowell and second baseman Jerry Browne.

"We're a much more competitive team," Grieve said. "We thought we would have to make trades with our pitching staff to help our offense. But as it turned out, we're stronger offensively with the addition of Palmeiro and Franco, and we have a stronger starting staff with the addition of Ryan and Jamie Moyer taking Paul Kilgus' place.

"Our bullpen is a little shaky without Mitch (Williams), but I think our 10-man staff will be at least as good as last year's and our offense is better. Time will tell if that is true."

Grieve's deals caught the eye of Oakland manager Tony LaRussa, whose A's finished 33½ games ahead of Texas in the American League West last season.

"I think it's obvious nobody is going to concede the division to the A's," LaRussa said. "Texas has improved itself tremendously."

An apparent breakdown in the relationship between Ryan and Astros owner John McMullen enabled the Rangers to sign the 41-year-old righthander. Ryan will get a $200,000 signing bonus, $1.6 million in salary in 1989 and a $200,000 buyout if the Rangers do not exercise a 1990 option for $1.4 million.

Ryan became the third player in a span of eight days to surpass Charlie Hough, who had been the best-paid player in club history. First, free agent shortstop Scott Fletcher re-signed for a $1.2 million salary in a three-year package for $3.975 million. Then, Grieve traded for Franco, who came from Cleveland with a $1.225 million salary.

The signing of Ryan put the biggest smile on the face of manager Bobby Valentine.

"To date, this is the one most important transaction the Texas Rangers have ever made," Valentine said. "Very simply, that is because Nolan Ryan is not only as fine a performer but as fine a human being as any organization could have associated with it."

> "To date, this is the one most important transaction the Texas Rangers have ever made," Valentine said. "Very simply, that is because Nolan Ryan is not only as fine a performer but as fine a human being as any organization could have associated with it."

While a potential payoff of $3.2 million was a lure, Ryan said he was drawn to the Rangers by a desire to be close to his home in Alvin, Texas, about 25 miles south of Houston.

"I am a die-hard Texan," Ryan said. "I really wanted to remain in Texas."

McMullen said Ryan's decision was based only on a high state income tax in California, not on Ryan's loyalties to his home state.

"The reason they (the California Angels) didn't get him was the difference in taxes," McMullen said. "It was a totally monetary decision."

RYAN EXPRESS (15KS) STILL ROLLING AT 42

by PHIL ROGERS   **APRIL 24, 1989**

ARLINGTON—It took Nolan Ryan only two starts with the Texas Rangers to break the club's strikeout record and put together a serious bid for the sixth no-hitter of his career.

Ryan retired the first 20 hitters April 12 at Milwaukee before walking Robin Yount. He took his no-hitter into the eighth inning before Terry Francona lined an opposite-field single into left field with none out and Glenn Braggs on base via a walk.

With the temperature 44 degrees and dropping at game time, Ryan struck out 15 batters, including 13 of the first 19 he faced. This was evidence that the Ryan Express is still rolling at age 42.

"What's amazing is that he had no curveball all night," said Milwaukee right fielder Rob Deer, who struck out twice. "He couldn't get his curveball over. When he does, I hear he's really unhittable."

Ryan got the next three batters after Francona's hit in the eighth and left the game, having thrown 134 pitches. Craig McMurtry gave up three hits and a run in the ninth as the Rangers won, 8-1.

Ryan threw 95 fastballs, the best of which registered at 97-98 mph on the JUGS gun. He got only one strike on the 11 curveballs he tried, but had control of his change up, throwing 19 of 28 for strikes.

"I think I've had better stuff," said Ryan, who raised his record career strikeout total to 4,798.

When manager Bobby Valentine pulled Ryan after the eighth inning, it cost Ryan a shot at the 56th shutout of his career, but that was no issue. Ryan had been bothered by leg problems in spring training and lasted only five innings in his debut for the Rangers April 6 against Detroit. Against the Brewers, his pitch total was climbing beyond the preferred range, but Valentine was not about to yank Ryan when he had a chance to add to his record of five no-hitters.

"He was going to keep throwing until they hit it," Valentine said.

Ryan should have been out of the seventh with his perfect game intact. Yount hit a foul pop-up on the first pitch, but there was miscommunication between first baseman Rafael Palmeiro and second baseman Julio Franco and the ball dropped between them. Yount took a 3-and-2 fastball at his knees for ball four.

Ryan struck out Deer to end the seventh and walked Braggs to start the eighth. Francona then stroked the first pitch, an outside fastball, over the head of third baseman Steve Buechele.

"As many times as I've been in that situation (a possible no-hitter), I'm realistic enough to not get too caught up in it," Ryan said. "The last six outs are the toughest outs."

The 15 strikeouts by Ryan broke the Texas single-game record of 14 that was shared by Jim Bibby and Bert Blyleven, the only pitchers to throw no-hitters for the Rangers.

Ryan hasn't had a no-hitter since he surpassed Sandy Koufax with his record No. 5 for Houston against Los Angeles on September 26, 1981. He had four no-hitters for the Angels—two in 1973, one in '74 and another in '75. Since 1981, he's had a few close calls. On April 27, 1988, pitching for Houston, he lost a no-hitter against Philadelphia on a one-out single in the ninth by Mike Schmidt.

"I'd like to throw another no-hitter," Ryan said. "But my attitude about it is, 'If it happens, that's fine.' But it's not something you can work toward."

RYAN HEADS FOR 5,000 K'S, AND MAYBE NO-NO

by PHIL ROGERS

JULY 10, 1989

ARLINGTON—Nolan Ryan keeps inching toward a landmark 5,000th career strikeout while almost regularly watching a sixth career no-hitter slip away.

Ryan, the only major leaguer ever to throw five no-hitters, took a no-hitter into the eighth inning three times in his first 15 starts with the Texas Rangers. His bid June 25 for No. 6 died when right fielder Ruben Sierra lost sight of a sinking line drive hit by Cleveland's Brook Jacoby with two out in the eighth.

"It's just another example of how the last six outs are usually the toughest," Ryan said. "That's one of the reasons I don't get really too up about it until the ninth."

Ryan, 42, held Milwaukee hitless for seven innings April 12 before giving up an opposite-field single to Terry Francona. On April 23, he went 8⅓ innings in Toronto before Nelson Liriano tripled.

Ryan closed out his one-hitter against the Blue Jays and added the 11th of his career June 3 in Seattle when he gave up a leadoff single to Harold Reynolds, then retired 27 in a row.

At Arlington Stadium on June 25, Ryan pitched five perfect innings before walking Jacoby to start the sixth. He kept a Sunday night crowd of 23,606 hanging on every pitch until Jacoby's drive in the eighth landed at the feet of Sierra for a single.

"I feel bad," said Sierra, who gave chase until he lost the ball in the stadium lights. "I want him to throw the no-hitter. I was going to dive, but if I can't see it, I can't dive."

Ryan let Sierra off the hook by giving up two hits in the ninth, including Dave Clark's home run.

Manager Bobby Valentine believes the odds are turning in Ryan's favor for a sixth no-hitter.

"Nolan's great, isn't he?" said Valentine. "If he keeps pitching like that, he'll win a lot of games—and get a no-hitter, too."

Although the no-hitter got away, Ryan recorded his 4,900th strikeout when he fanned Joe Carter in the fourth inning. At his 1989 pace of 8.5 strikeouts per start, Ryan figured to reach 5,000 in his 27th start, which should come about September 1.

"The only one that has any meaning to it is 5,000," Ryan said. "I want to do that. The 4,900th only means I'm 100 away."

And gaining.

> **"It's just another example of how the last six outs are usually the toughest," Ryan said. "That's one of the reasons I don't get really too up about it until the ninth."**

5,000 SOUNDS GOOD TO RYAN

King of Ks Putting Up Total That May Never Be Touched

by PHIL ROGERS   AUGUST 21, 1989

ARLINGTON—It was 7 o'clock in the morning, and the Texas Rangers were scheduled to play at Cleveland Stadium that April afternoon. They had played a night game the day before. Yet there was Tom House in the elevator of the tower at Stouffer's on the Square, rubbing sleep from his eyes and trying to get set for his day while descending to the lobby.

House was on his way to meet Nolan Ryan for a workout at the Cleveland Athletic Club. For a strange moment, he thought maybe he was dreaming.

Here's a pitching coach on his way to meet one of his pitchers, a certain Hall of Famer, to lift weights and speak the language of the game they have both loved since childhood. And it's 7 a.m.?

> ## "I was told you're nobody until you do, but I still don't like it."
> *John Olerud, on becoming the 1,079th player to be struck out by Nolan Ryan*

"I'm thinking, 'It's 7 in the morning, we played a game last night and I'm going down to meet Nolan Ryan to lift weights. What's wrong with this picture?'" House said. "Well, nothing's wrong with it. Now that I've gotten to know Nolan, I know that's just the way he is. I realize that's why he's still throwing as hard as he is at age 42. He does what it takes to prepare himself, no matter what that is."

Ryan became the major leagues' oldest player when Tommy John was released by the New York Yankees on Memorial Day. While other athletes from Ryan's generation have been absorbed back into mainstream America, he continues to put up records that may never be matched.

Ryan's latest milestone is 5,000 strikeouts, which he has been marching steadily toward since he fanned Montreal's Brad Mills on April 27, 1983, to replace Walter Johnson as baseball's strikeout king.

Ryan, a $2 million free agent, entered his first season with the Texas Rangers needing 225 strikeouts to reach 5,000, which figured to be a full season of work—if it could be achieved at all this year. He had struck out that many only three times in the previous 10 seasons.

But Ryan has led the American League in strikeouts continually since he whiffed 15 Milwaukee Brewers on a 44-degree night April 12 at County Stadium.

He struck out at least 10 batters in 12 of his first 23 starts, which left him just 14 short of the milestone. He figured to reach No. 5,000 during the Rangers' six-game home stand against Oakland and California August 22-27.

While Pete Rose had become a stats freak and singles hitter by the time he amassed his 4,192nd hit, breaking Ty Cobb's record, Ryan was more a twin of his younger version than a shadow in this season of the 5,000th strikeout.

Through August 10, he was not only leading the Rangers with 13 victories but had held the opposition to a .187 batting average, a figure that led the league.

Ryan finished his 22nd major league season with 288 strikeouts, his highest total since he struck out 341 in 1977. His average of 11.1 strikeouts per nine innings was better than the ratio (10.6) he had when he set a major league single-season record with 383 strikeouts for the Angels in 1973.

But Ryan's current strikeout pace still pales in comparison to his minor league days in the New York Mets' organization. Before becoming a major leaguer for good at age 21 in 1968, Ryan racked up 445 strikeouts in 291 innings—an average of 14 per nine innings. The Express was rolling.

Imagine the reaction of hitters to one of Ryan's most closely kept secrets—that he was never trying to strike them out.

"I think a lot of people think I really tried to strike out people, and that's not the case," Ryan said. "I was just always a strikeout-style pitcher. That's what my stuff made me, not what I tried to become. I never went out with the idea of striking out people.

"The only time I ever thought about a strikeout is when I got two strikes on a hitter in a situation where the team needed a strikeout.

"The style of pitcher I am, I get a lot of swings and misses. That's why I get so many more strikeouts than other people. My really high totals come when hitters are looking for my fastball and I'm getting my breaking ball over the plate. I'm going to have more strikeouts than other pitchers do, because of my breaking ball. Any time you have a high strikeout total, it's because you have a quality breaking ball.

"Going back through history, all of the strikeout pitchers had really good breaking balls—Bob Feller,

MILESTONE K'S FOR RYAN

Milestone strikeouts in the career of Nolan Ryan

No.	Date	Opponent
1	Sept. 11, 1966	Pat Jarvis, Atlanta
100	June 18, 1968	Denny Lemaster, Houston
500	April 18, 1972	Charlie Manuel, Minnesota
1000	July 3, 1973	Sal Bando, Oakland
1500	August 25, 1974	Sandy Alomar, N.Y. Yankees
2000	August 31, 1976	Ron LeFlore, Detroit
2500	August 12, 1978	Buddy Bell, Cleveland
3000	July 4, 1980	Cesar Geronimo, Cincinnati
3500	April 17, 1983	Andre Dawson, Montreal
*3509	April 27, 1983	Brad Mills, Montreal
4000	July 11, 1985	Danny Heep, N.Y. Mets
4500	Sept. 9, 1987	Mike Aldrete, San Francisco

*Strikeout No. 3509 broke Walter Johnson's existing career record of 3508.

Louis DeLuca

Ryan, famous for his exercise regimen, works out at the Rangers' facility.

Bob Gibson, Steve Carlton, Tom Seaver. They all had exceptionally good breaking balls.

"Of all the 300-strikeout guys, the 3,000 guys, the only one of them that didn't have an exceptionally good breaking ball was Gaylord Perry, and he had other pitches. He pitched a tremendous amount of innings."

Ryan often has little recall about games in which he has pitched.

"Sometimes," he said, "I can't tell you who the hitters were, even if you asked me right after a game."

But some strikeouts stick out in his mind. Among them:

STRIKEOUT TOP 10

The top 10 in major league history in career strikeouts.

1.	NOLAN RYAN	*4,986
2.	Steve Carlton	4,136
3.	Tom Seaver	3,640
4.	Don Sutton	3,574
5.	Gaylord Perry	3,534
6.	Bert Blyleven	*3,526
7.	Walter Johnson	3,508
8.	Phil Niekro	3,342
9.	Ferguson Jenkins	3,192
10.	Bob Gibson	3,117

*Pitcher still active; total through August 10, 1989

• The first—Atlanta pitcher Pat Jarvis, on September 11, 1966 (when Ryan made his first appearance with the Mets, relieving in an 8-3 loss to the Braves). "I've read that was it," Ryan said.

• The last out of his lone World Series appearance—Paul Blair of Baltimore, in Game 4 of the 1969 Series.

"I don't think I realized how fortunate we were," Ryan said. "As a young player, you just take for granted that those things happen so often."

• His record 383rd in 1973—Rich Reese of Minnesota fanned in the 11th inning September 27 as Ryan went the distance for the Angels to gain a

Ryan talks with George W. Bush, general partner of the Texas Rangers.

Louis DeLuca

5-4 victory that lifted his record to 21-16. The strikeout enabled Ryan to surpass Sandy Koufax's one-season record of 382 in 1965.

"A fastball," Ryan said of the pitch that retired Reese.

•   The last out in his fourth no-hitter—Bobby Grich of Baltimore was the victim on June 1, 1975.

"A changeup," Ryan said of the pitch that brought him his last American League no-hitter.

•   The record 3,509th—Montreal's Mills in that game in 1983, when Ryan was pitching for the Houston Astros.

"At the time, I wanted to be the first (to surpass Johnson's career total of 3,508 strikeouts)," Ryan said. "My feelings at the time were that two or three guys had a very good shot at it."

Ryan admitted to an anticipation about No. 5,000.

"I would like to achieve that because nobody has ever reached that number," Ryan said. "It's just a number, but it's like 20 wins. What's so different about 20 wins and 19 wins? Twenty wins just means a lot more for your reputation than winning 19 games. Five thousand is a number that sounds good."

Ryan's strikeout record is to pitchers what Rose's record is for hitters. Both may be eventually caught, but it's hard to picture the player who can combine talent with durability better than Rose or Ryan have.

"I don't have any idea which would fall first," Ryan said, "the strikeout record or the hit record. It's a possibility somebody could surpass the strikeout record.

"There are a lot of pitchers out there now who have a shot at 3,000. But after you get 3,000, that's when it gets tough. You have to stay healthy, have to pitch a lot of innings, a lot of years and maintain your stuff. That's the toughest part—maintaining your stuff."

Ryan's fastball hit 100 mph at its peak, when he was winning 62 games in a three-year span with California from 1972 through 1974. The Rangers have clocked him at 97 this year, and he is consistently around 95 mph.

Ryan's pitching was no side show, either. Through August 10, the Rangers had played at a .654 winning percentage with him starting (15-8), while playing a .500 pace (45-45) with anyone else starting.

Texas won 12 of Ryan's 17 starts before the All-Star break, and he often seemed to be holding to-

gether a staff that was ready to disintegrate.

Bobby Witt struggled to establish his velocity, Jamie Moyer was lost for most of the season with a pulled muscle in his shoulder and Charlie Hough's knuckleball was a tempting treat for hitters as he battled through shoulder tendinitis.

Ryan rode to the rescue, pitching well enough that many thought he was a deserving choice to start the All-Star Game. As it was, he followed Oakland's Dave Stewart into the July 11 game in Anaheim and earned his first victory in seven trips to the midsummer classic.

"He was irreplaceable to our effort," Rangers manager Bobby Valentine said. "The way everything started, and with what happened to Witt, Hough and Moyer in the first half, having Nolan was the greatest thing that could happen to our team. There's not enough words to express it."

Ryan hadn't won more than 12 games in a season since 1982, going 68-67 in his last six years with the Astros. But he got No. 13 on August 10, in the Rangers' 113th game.

Ryan credits his new team for his improved record. While the Astros failed to average as many as four runs per game in Ryan's starts from 1985 through '88, the Rangers averaged 4.6 runs in his first 23 starts. They scored five or more runs 10 times.

How many games would he have won two years ago with that support? His 2.76 ERA in '87 led the National League, but he won only eight of 34 starts.

"The most frustrating thing in my career was being on bad teams," said Ryan, who had improved his career record to 286-260 with his strong start in Texas. "I would have been pitching to win 'em. That was frustrating."

Ryan believes the challenge of establishing his greatness with a new team was good for him.

"Sometimes you don't realize it, but you get into a rut," Ryan said.

"It's been a nice change for me, and been a nice change for my family. We've enjoyed it."

Ryan has often seemed to overmatch American Leaguers who come to the plate looking strictly for the fastball they have heard so much about.

"Early in the year, I had a good command of my curveball and changeup," Ryan said. "I was facing a lot of hitters who hadn't seen me and were looking for my fastball."

He tricked many with a changeup that he didn't throw during his first term in the A.L. He credits Joe Nuxhall, the former Cincinnati lefthander and now a broadcaster for the Reds, with helping him develop the pitch during the 50-day players' strike in 1981.

"The difference in me the last seven or eight years is the changeup coming into play," said Ryan. "I think the changeup has made my fastball more effective. On nights when I don't have a good curveball, it keeps hitters from sitting on the fastball. That's helped me pitch more innings, so I struck out more people.

"When hitters are seeing me for the first time who don't know me, they go to the plate with the preconceived idea they're going to see fastballs. Until you see my changeup, curveball, you don't realize how important they are to me. But I don't think it takes hitters long to adjust. They see me two or three at-bats and they pretty much know what I'm going to do. They've seen all the pitches, and have a better idea."

Ryan's only disappointment has been coming so close to his sixth no-hitter without putting it away. He lost potential no-hitters on an eighth-inning single by Milwaukee's Terry Francona on April 12, a ninth-inning triple by Toronto's Nelson Liriano on April 23, an eighth-inning double by Cleveland's Brook Jacoby on June 25 and a ninth-inning single by Detroit's Dave Bergman on August 10.

"Any time you get that close, it's hard to walk off the field and not be disappointed," said Ryan. "Now it's more disappointing than it was earlier in my career. Early in my career, I'd think that the opportunity would come around again. Now it

feels like every time I let it slip away it could be my last."

Ryan's success has been at the heart of unprecedented interest in the Texas franchise. Arlington Stadium attendance went over one million at the earliest date ever, June 29, and entering August was running about 250,000 ahead of last year's pace—enough of a difference to fill Dallas' Reunion Arena

The Sporting News

almost 14 times over. For only the second time in 11 years, the Rangers were outdrawing the Astros.

Even Houston marketing director Ted Haracz admitted he experienced an internal feeling of deflation when Ryan spurned Astros owner John McMullen and signed with Texas last December 7, ending a nine-year relationship with the Astros.

"I don't think anybody here enjoyed his departure," Haracz said. "Given everybody's druthers, we'd rather he had elected to stay here. A lot of people were down when he did sign with Texas, but it hasn't deterred us from doing our job."

With basketball's Rockets providing little to talk about, Ryan's decision dominated air time on talk shows in Houston during the winter and spring. It created an anti-McMullen climate that peaked when a fist fight broke out in a concourse of the Astrodome after ushers removed two fans carrying a placard criticizing McMullen.

It's not the first time a team that lost Ryan suffered a negative reaction. California's attendance fell off by more than 200,000 after the Angels lost Ryan to the Astros in 1980. That year, their first with Ryan, the Astros' attendance climbed from 1.9 million to 2.28 million.

"Our attendance is down, but it's down from the third-best year in our history," Haracz said. "He (Ryan) has had a fabulous year, and as a baseball fan you'd want to go see him pitch, but he had pitched here for 10 years (actually, nine). Some of his appeal had worn off here. It's a different situation than with the Rangers."

There's no sure way to quantify Ryan's dollar value to the Rangers. His 13 starts in Arlington had drawn about 2,200 more fans per game than the average with Texas' other pitchers starting.

Perhaps the best example of his drawing power: 25,735 came to see his first start in a Texas uniform, despite a 5 p.m. start for that April 6 game; a Monday-night record crowd of 38,274 saw his rematch with Milwaukee on April 17, five days after his near no-hitter at County Stadium; a Wednesday doubleheader with California on June 14 drew a sellout crowd of 40,159 with Ryan and Hough starting.

The Rangers, who have never drawn more than 1,763,053 in a season, were on pace through August 9 to go over 2.2 million. They set a record with season-ticket sales in excess of 7,000. Fort Worth-based WBAP, which paid almost twice its previous rights fee to retain the Rangers last winter, has increased the network of stations carrying its broadcast from 16 to 25, including stations in San Antonio and Houston.

Before KSEV opted to go head-to-head with the Astros, no Houston stations had ever carried Rangers games.

How much of that is a result of Ryan's presence?

"Probably 100 percent," said WBAP sales manager Chris Leiss. "New players like (Rafael) Palmeiro and (Julio) Franco play into it, but I'd say most of the new interest has been because of Ryan."

Leiss said it was no longer as tough to sell commercial time during the broadcasts. "Our sales are up significantly, to a record level," he said. "We've never done close to what we've done this year, and it really starting exploding the day Nolan Ryan decided to join the Texas Rangers."

Has anyone ever pitched as long and stayed as healthy as Ryan? It's doubtful.

While the unnatural act of firing a baseball in ways designed to keep it from being hit seems to take its toll on the shoulders and elbows of men closer to the age of Ryan's oldest son, 17-year-old Reid, Ryan just keeps rolling.

In 25 professional seasons, he's had surgery once (bone chips were removed from his elbow in 1975) and has been on the disabled list just six times, mostly with pulled muscles in his legs.

"I can't give one reason as to why I've been able to do this for so long," Ryan said. "I think mechanics and body type play a big role. I do know the older you get, the more important conditioning becomes."

Ryan never seems to sit in the clubhouse. He always seems to be riding the stationary bike, working in the weight room or performing stretching exercises.

"He's like the mailman," House said. "Nothing keeps him from making his rounds. I don't think the general public is aware of the effort he puts in."

Gene Coleman, a former consultant to the National Aeronautics and Space Administration who helped Ryan refine his workouts, was amazed at the extent of Ryan's routine when Ryan joined the Astros in 1980.

"Nobody else was doing it," Coleman said. "But when you go through the league, the guys doing the most (conditioning) work had the best longevity— Carlton, the Niekros (Phil and Joe), Don Sutton, Seaver, Burt Hooton and Ryan.

"Guys coming in as youngsters and losing velocity, they weren't doing as much work.

"People say that Nolan Ryan and Tom Seaver would have been successful anyway, and they probably could have been, but they wouldn't have had the longevity they've had."

Ryan was among the first pitchers to begin lifting heavy weights. He began by sneaking down to the weight room at Anaheim Stadium in 1972, and his 19 victories that season enabled him to gradually reveal some of his secrets.

"It's weight conditioning, not weight lifting," he said. "I'm not trying to see how much weight I can lift; I'm trying to lift the right weights in the right way."

With age, Ryan has cut down on his running. Much of his running last winter was done underwater, in the deep end of a swimming pool while he wore an oxygen mask and snorkel.

Coleman said that the exercise in the pool provides endurance without wear and tear.

"His feet never touch the ground, and the resistance to water is 12 times the resistance to air," Coleman said. "He has less residual soreness."

Ryan's work ethic was instilled at an early age. As he grew up in Alvin, Texas, he would rise in the middle of the night and help his father make his rounds delivering the *Houston Post.*

It was just something that was necessary, like all the off-field hours that go into every inning he pitches.

"I don't think I came to a conclusion one day that for me to be successful I was going to have to work extremely hard," Ryan said. "Basically that's been my approach to anything I've ever done. I never want to walk off the field feeling I got beat because the other guys are in better shape than I am. That's something you have direct control over."

Ryan's contract with the Rangers contains a club option for 1989, but Ryan has said he won't decide about pitching another year until after this season, when he gathers his wife and three children around for a discussion.

He said he would have retired after last season if his family had preferred having him around the house more. A protracted lockout or player strike in 1990 also could end his career.

"Only Nolan knows if he's reached the point where the amount of work necessary to support his fastball is too much," House said. "Only Nolan knows when his fastball isn't right. But I would be very disappointed if he didn't play next year, and not just because of the numbers he puts up for the Texas Rangers. It would be because of the contributions he makes as a person and as a friend. I enjoy being around him."

Watching Ryan compete on a pitcher's mound has given House an insight to one of the most remarkable careers ever in baseball.

"The enjoyment he gets by pitching a baseball is worth all the work, all the people pulling at him, all the effort that goes into preparing himself," House said. "It must be akin to what an actor feels when he gets on stage, or like a comedian when he gets a laugh. It's what he lives to do, and what he loves to do."

The Sporting News

The Sporting News

> **"It gave me no chance. He just blew it by me. But it's an honor. I'll have another paragraph in all the baseball books. I'm already in the books three or four times."**
>
> *Rickey Henderson on the fastball that made him Nolan Ryan's 5,000th strikeout victim.*

Strikeout number 5,000, vs. Rickey Henderson.

Louis DeLuca

RYAN IS DISABLED WITH BACK SPASMS

JUNE 4, 1990

Back spasms forced Texas Rangers pitcher Nolan Ryan onto the 15-day disabled list May 24, retroactive to May 18. The 43-year-old Ryan initially opposed the move, thinking he could return sooner than the first week in June, but then realized that the back problem had lingered for three consecutive starts. He returned to Houston to work with Ronald Slaughter, a chiropractor. "Nolan's such a competitor that no one wants to be out there more," manager Bobby Valentine said. "This way, we know he'll take the extra time he needs. The plan all along was to have him ready to play for the long haul." Ryan made all 32 of his scheduled starts last year. He was 4-2 with a 4.26 earned-run average when he went on the disabled list. He was seven victories short of 300 in his career.

THE RUB ON RYAN'S NO-HITTER: COULD BACK PAIN BE A SIGNAL THAT THE END OF A LONG CAREER IS NEAR?

by PHIL ROGERS   **JUNE 25, 1990**

OAKLAND—Reese Ryan rubbed his father's back between innings of the Texas Rangers-Oakland Athletics game June 11. It was the gesture of a 14-year-old boy prompted by both affection and concern. But for those who witnessed the exchange between father and son, it became a personal signature on Nolan Ryan's sixth no-hitter.

"He told me it felt OK," said Reese. "Then after the eighth, he just came back, looked at me and smiled. I think he knew he was going to do it."

Ryan, 43, extended the boundary of his legend out into baseball's stratosphere that night, using his fastball and a wicked change up to overpower the defending world-champion A's. He struck out 14 and walked two in becoming, among other things, the first major league pitcher to throw no-hitters in three decades (1970s, '80s and '90s.)

"The thing I'll get chills about wasn't the last out or any out in the ninth," said Rangers manager Bobby Valentine. "The scene I'll remember is Nolan on the bench with his son rubbing his back and patting him on the leg, giving him a pep talk. No

> **"The thing I'll get chills about wasn't the last out or any out in the ninth," said Rangers manager Bobby Valentine. "The scene I'll remember is Nolan on the bench with his son rubbing his back and patting him on the leg, giving him a pep talk. No one else could bear to talk to him. That was a wonderful sight."**

one else could bear to talk to him. That was a wonderful sight."

Oakland manager Tony LaRussa was among those amazed by Ryan's ability to throw a no-hitter while battling sharp pains in his back. Ryan, who was making only his second start since coming off the 15-day disabled list, said the back spasms were "about the same" as when he went on the D.L. on May 24 (retroactive to May 18).

"He flinched and grimaced on a few pitches," LaRussa said. "He pitched with pain and still was great. That's what makes him even greater, to do all that in discomfort."

A's hitting instructor Merv Rettenmund said, "They should just open the doors of the Hall of Fame and put him in right now. He belongs there. He shouldn't have to wait five years."

Ryan had lasted only five innings in the previous start, also against Oakland, since his ninth career stay on the disabled list. He never really felt comfortable physically during the no-hitter.

"I was concerned with my back problems, and I said, 'Well, I'll just go seven innings,'" Ryan said.

"Then, I got through the seventh and I decided I'm not going to give in to it, because I just needed six more outs."

Ryan flirted with his sixth no-hitter six times in 32 starts with Texas last year, twice losing opportunities in the ninth inning. This time, he turned up the heat. His fastball, which had not been clocked over 90 mph in the first seven innings, hit 95 on the Athletics' radar gun in the ninth.

He struck out five of the last eight hitters, getting the final two outs on shortstop Jeff Huson's good play on a dribbler by Rickey Henderson and right fielder Ruben Sierra's catch of a foul fly by Willie Randolph.

Ryan had waited for his sixth no-hitter since September 26, 1981. Then, pitching for the Houston Astros, he eclipsed Sandy Koufax's major league

NO COMMON DENOMINATOR—EXCEPT RYAN

Anyone in search of a mystical pattern to the record six no-hitters hurled by Nolan Ryan may be left scratching his head. Consider ...

- Three of the no-hitters were at home, three were on the road.
- Six different catchers caught the six different games.
- Six different teams (five American League and one National League) were the victims.
- In outings immediately prior to his no-hitters, Ryan was the losing pitcher on four of six occasions.
- One no-hitter came in May, two in June, one in July and two in September.
- Ryan wore three different uniforms—the California Angels (four times), Houston Astros and Texas Rangers—in setting the record.

record of four no-hitters with a 5-0 victory over Los Angeles in the Astrodome.

"The longer you go, the more you wonder if you left that part of your game behind you," Ryan admitted after authoring No. 6. "And it was neat that Reese was on the bench with me. He was nervous about talking to me, and I had to get a kick out of that."

Reese Ryan was not the only one nervous about his dad's back. Two days after the no-hitter, Ryan left the Rangers and went to Los Angeles for a full physical exam. Dr. Lewis Yocum, the California Angels' team doctor, discovered a stress fracture in Ryan's lower vertebrae. Yocum said the injury was in the healing stage and gave Ryan a cortisone shot to help with the recovery.

"At least we know what we're dealing with,"

June 11, 1990
TEXAS 5, OAKLAND 0

TEXAS	ab	r	h	bi	OAKLAND	ab	r	h	bi
Pettis cf	5	1	2	0	R. Henderson lf	4	0	0	0
Palmeiro 1b	4	1	0	0	Randolph 2b	4	0	0	0
Franco 2b	4	2	2	4	Jennings 1b	3	0	0	0
Sierra rf	3	0	1	0	Hassey dh	3	0	0	0
Baines dh	4	0	1	0	Jose rf	3	0	0	0
Incaviglia lf	4	0	1	0	D. Henderson cf	3	0	0	0
Jo Russell c	3	1	1	1	Quirk c	2	0	0	0
Buechele 3b	4	0	0	0	Lansford ph	1	0	0	0
Huson ss	3	0	1	0	Steinbach c	0	0	0	0
					Weiss ss	2	0	0	0
					Gallego 3b	1	0	0	0
					Phelps ph	1	0	0	0
TOTALS	34	5	9	5		27	0	0	0

```
Texas      2 1 0    0 2 0    0 0 0—5
Oakland    0 0 0    0 0 0    0 0 0—0
```

LOB—Texas 6, Oakland 2. HR—Franco 2 (6), Jo Russell (2). SB—Pettis, Sierra, Weiss.

TEXAS	IP	H	R	ER	BB	SO
Ryan (W 5-3)	9	0	0	0	2	14
OAKLAND						
Sanderson (L 7-3)	6	8	5	5	2	3
Norris	2	1	0	0	2	3
Nelson	1	0	0	0	0	0

said Ryan, who appeared relieved. "It helps that he told me this is something that is going to get better."

Back problems have ended the careers of many pitchers. Allie Reynolds, one of only 20 other major leaguers to pitch more than one no-hitter, had to call it quits after the 1954 season, at age 39, because of back spasms similar to the ones that put Ryan on the disabled list.

"I hate to say it, but that means the end is near," Reynolds said. "That's a terrific pain to put up with. I attempted to (pitch with it). The pain got so bad I couldn't put up with it. When your muscles start to spasm, it means you've just about used 'em up. God knows he has thrown a whole lot more than I did."

But this spring Ryan negotiated a contract extension that will pay him $3.3 million if he returns for the 1991 season. And Rangers pitching coach Tom House expects he'll be back.

"I think if you look back at his career, he's had problems before and adjusted," House said. "He did it with a bad elbow (in 1986). He figures out how to handle it. He's amazing in that way. A lot of pitchers compensate the wrong way and end up hurting something else."

Ryan's wife, Ruth, and their daughter, Wendy, were also at the Oakland Coliseum to witness no-hitter No. 6.

"Not a bad family outing, was it?" said Ruth.

The Ryans' post-game celebration was typically low-key. There were two hours of interviews before Ryan could even get away to do his normal workout on a stationary bike. By the time he and his family returned to the hotel, it was past midnight.

"We called Domino's (pizza)," Ryan said. "I didn't have much choice. Everything (else) was closed."

AP/Wide World Photos

The zeros on the scoreboard tell the story as Ryan chugs along during his sixth career no-hitter.

AMAZIN' NOLAN KEEPS ON ROLLIN'

by CRAIG CARTER **JUNE 25, 1990**

As if there were any need for further reason to marvel at Nolan Ryan's pitching accomplishments, consider some of these sidelights that came packaged with his sixth no-hitter, on June 11, against the Oakland A's:

He now is the oldest pitcher—by more than two years—to hurl a no-hitter in a major league game.

He has averaged 13 strikeouts in those six no-hitters. (Only seven other pitchers have collected as many as 13 strikeouts in any no-hit game.)

He is the only pitcher to throw no-hitters in three different decades and the first pitcher since Cleveland's Dick Bosman, in 1974, to throw a no-hitter against a defending league champion.

His sixth no-hitter came 17 years and 27 days after his first gem, by far the longest span in big-league history. (Bob Feller had an 11-year, two-month, 15-day span between his first and last.)

No-hit addendum: Ryan's manager with the Texas Rangers, Bobby Valentine, was a team-mate when Ryan threw his first no-hitter. Valentine played center field for the California Angels on May 15, 1973.

There are only six active major leaguers, aside from Ryan himself, who made appearances in any of his first five no-hitters. They are Pedro Guerrero, Mike Scioscia, Ted Power and Dave Stewart, who played for the Dodgers, and Terry Puhl and Denny Walling, who were with the Astros, when Ryan pitched his fifth no-hitter, against Los Angeles, on September 26, 1981.

The 1990 season, which already has witnessed no-hitters by Ryan, Seattle's Randy Johnson and a combination job by California's Mark Langston and Mike Witt, marks the first time since 1977 that three no-hitters have been thrown in one league in one season. That year, Kansas City's Jim Colburn, Cleveland's Dennis Eckersley and Texas' Bert Blyleven turned the trick.

RANGERS' STAR AN ICON IN THE HEART OF TEXAS

by JOE GERGEN **AUGUST 6, 1990**

ARLINGTON—Of all the tall tales spawned in this sprawling state, the saga of Nolan Ryan is among the most improbable. Yet, happily for the man and his fellow Texans, all of it is true. Always at home on the range, Ryan was destined to make history on the mound.

The youngster from the small town of Alvin who generated such little interest a quarter of a century ago has evolved into a billboard-sized attraction.

Moreover, as the most prominent professional athlete in the Lone Star State, Ryan has elevated baseball—which once ranked behind football and spring football in priorities—to a prominent position in the region's consciousness.

"He's made the image of baseball No. 1 down here," said Red Murff, the scout who signed Ryan out of high school in 1965. "He grew up in a football area, but now even football people think he's the greatest."

Indeed, when he jogged out of the dugout at Arlington Stadium July 25, there were few Texans, from Brownsville to Amarillo, who were unmoved by his quest. Twenty-two years and three months after his first major-league triumph, on behalf of the New York Mets in Houston, he was presented with the opportunity to win his 300th game in his home state against the other New York team, the Yankees.

Emotionally, of course, Ryan never left Texas, although his professional itinerary took him to the east and west coasts. He always maintained a home in Alvin and has expanded his roots to include a summer residence here and a working ranch near San Antonio.

"You travel around Texas with me, and everyone wants to talk about Nolan Ryan," said George W. Bush, the President's son and the general partner in the ballclub. "If you polled the people, he'd be the biggest celebrity in Texas by far."

Big enough to sell out the ballpark in each of his last four starts. Big enough to inspire a rash of banners, including one that identified the team as the Texas Ryangers. Big enough to draw the likes of commissioner Fay Vincent and American League president Bobby Brown to the stadium for what promised to be an historic occasion.

Alas, Ryan suffered through his most difficult start of the season. He was battered for 10 hits, including three homers, and charged with seven runs in eight innings. The Rangers rallied to tie the score with two outs in the ninth and eventually defeated the Yankees, 9-7, in 11 innings—after Ryan had showered and dressed.

Typically, the man was less disappointed for himself than for the relatives and many friends who had gathered here to celebrate a milestone. "I can honestly say I wanted to win this game worse than any other this year," he said, "because so many people interrupted their lives to share it with me. They came from all over the country."

The lure was baseball's midseason gift to itself, a special night for a good man. "Good things ought to happen to Nolan Ryan," Murff said. "He's a nice person."

Murff, a resident of Brenham, was in a better position than most to know. He was a virtual one-man rooting section at a time when other major league organizations, as well as his front office in New York, were unimpressed by Ryan's potential. That he was the 295th player selected in the 1965 amateur draft is part of the legend that contributes to Ryan's standing today. Remarkably, if it hadn't been for Murff, the man who has amassed more strikeouts and thrown more no-hitters than anyone in history might not have been drafted at all.

Even the lowly Colt .45s, the expansion franchise located 25 miles north of Ryan's hometown, weren't interested. "To my knowledge, (former Houston general manager) Paul Richards never saw me pitch," Ryan said. "I know a Houston scout saw me, but I never heard from them. I only weighed 150 pounds in high school, and a lot of people didn't like me because of my build. Where Red Murff was different was he met with my parents. He saw how big my dad was. He saw my genetic potential. He did his homework."

4TH SELLOUT, NO 300 FOR THE MEAL TICKET
August 6, 1990

Nolan Ryan's bid for victory No. 300 demonstrated his role as the Texas Rangers' meal ticket the last two seasons. His July 25 start against the Yankees attracted a crowd of 41,954, largest of the year at Arlington Stadium. This was the fourth consecutive sellout for a game in which Ryan pitched. Through July 25, the Rangers' average attendance at home was 33,494 with Ryan starting and 23,758 with anyone else starting. "Nolan means more to us than money," Rangers President Mike Stone told the *Dallas Times Herald*. "It's ridiculous to try to establish the economic impact Nolan has." Last year, the Rangers averaged 28,420 with Ryan pitching, 25,602 without him…The Rangers marketed 300-win T-shirts, pennants and game programs July 25, but Ryan wasn't involved in the decision. "Nolan Ryan merchandise is always hopping," said Stephen Newhart, area general manager for ARA Leisure Services.

It's true, Murff said, that he did size up Ryan's father, who was taller than six feet and weighed 240 pounds. But it was the arm that mesmerized the scout. He first saw Ryan pitch, entirely by accident, on a Saturday afternoon in Ryan's sophomore year at Alvin High School. Murff was en route from an assignment in Galveston to another in Houston when he decided to stop at Alvin.

"I didn't know anything about him until I walked into the ball park," the scout recalled. "They were changing pitchers. Ryan's first two pitches were fastballs close to 100 miles per hour. I thought, "Good God, this is some kind of arm. Then he threw a terrible curve about 67 or 68 miles per hour, and the hitter doubled into right-center."

The previous night, Murff had watched Turk Farrell duel Jim Maloney of the Cincinnati Reds at old Colt Stadium. They were two of the premier power pitchers in the National League. "On my first report (on Ryan) to the front office, I put, 'Throws harder than Maloney and Farrell. Best arm I've ever seen in my life,'" Murff recalled.

With the permission of Ryan's coach, a former football player named Jim Watson, Murff began working with the young pitcher. And he assigned a friend and part-time scout, Red Gaskell, to attend every game in which Ryan was scheduled to pitch. By his senior year, however, Ryan's frame still hadn't filled out, he still didn't have a sharp curve and his lack of

RYAN'S 300TH DRAWS A CROWD IN ARLINGTON
August 13, 1990

Although the Rangers were playing at Milwaukee's County Stadium, 7,828 of their fans came to Arlington Stadium July 31 to watch Nolan Ryan's 300th victory. Team officials opened the stadium for only a $3 parking charge and showed the game on the Diamond Vision screen. The Rangers had pop fly-catching contests on the field and set up a speed gun in the bullpen. In addition, drawings were held to award baseballs every time a ball was fouled into the stands in Milwaukee. "With the crowd they got, they ought to do it more often," fan Wayne Mosby told the *Dallas Times Herald*. "I don't think I'll get a chance to see something like this again."

control was downright dangerous. The pitcher himself remembered a game in which he broke the batting helmet of the leadoff hitter and the arm of the second batter. "The third guy begged not to hit," he recalled.

But Murff continued to tell New York that this kid in Alvin was destined for greatness. Finally, Bing Devine, who had succeeded George Weiss as the Mets' general manager, flew to Houston for a look. Unfortunately, it wasn't Ryan's day to pitch. He wasn't rested, and he was anxious. He didn't make it through the third inning and left trailing, 7-0.

Ryan wasn't drafted until the eighth round, but at least he was picked. And the player and the scout, who now works in the same capacity for the Atlanta Braves, remain good friends and hunting companions to this day.

"I enjoy taking some small credit for Nolan Ryan," Murff said. "I feel good about it. I don't like to ride anybody's train, but if he lets me, I'll go along."

The journey will not be complete, of course, until Ryan arrives in Cooperstown. But it will be some time after that, Bush reasoned, that the full impact of the man will be felt in Texas. "This franchise hasn't had a tradition to pass on from one generation to the next," Bush said. "He will be our legacy, something for a man to tell his son or grandson—that he saw Nolan Ryan pitch."

> "You travel around Texas with me, and everyone wants to talk about Nolan Ryan," said George W. Bush, the President's son and the general partner in the ballclub. "If you polled the people, he'd be the biggest celebrity in Texas by far."

Louis DeLuca

Ryan waves to the crowd at Milwaukee's County Stadium after earning his 300th career victory.

RYAN'S SONG: LITTLE THINGS MEAN A LOT

by PHIL ROGERS   **AUGUST 13, 1990**

ARLINGTON—On a good day at the Astrodome, you could smell Nolan Ryan coming. He would be carrying a large box, filled with delicacies he had picked up in his hometown of Alvin, Texas, 20 miles south of Houston.

There would be 40 to 50 fried pies in the box. "Peach pies, lemon pies. He'd get them someplace in Alvin and bring them to the ballpark," said Houston Astros trainer Jim Ewell. "One day, Glenn Davis took four or five of 'em, and Nolan was disgusted. He said, 'Now I'm going to have to lock 'em away from Glenn so everybody gets one.'"

While raw power and stubborn longevity mark Ryan as baseball's newest 300-game winner, it's little things that make the man. Little things like honesty and consideration. Little things like sincerity and generosity.

"People who read about him in newspapers or a book tell you he can't be that good of a person," said Dave Oliver, third base coach of the Texas Rangers, for whom Ryan now pitches. "But if you're around him all the time, you know that's him."

Those regularly around Ryan were as relieved as he was when it took only two tries for Ryan to win his 300th game. Ryan's worst nightmare was that the quest would become "an ongoing thing," but those fears were laid to rest with an 11-3 victory in Milwaukee July 31.

"The last 15 days really have been as tough a 15 days as I've ever gone through," Ryan said afterward. "I didn't want this thing to go on."

Ryan, 27-14 in his two years with Texas, handled the demands from the media and fans graciously, as he usually does. In the end, the chase boiled down to home movies for the Ryan family.

Sons Reid, 18 and Reese, 14, were on the bench, in Rangers uniforms, when Ryan reached the milestone. They also spent part of the evening shooting video footage with a hand-held camera.

"I think it will be an enjoyable thing to take a look at and see what they came up with," Ryan said. "It's another event we got to experience as a family. Any time your family is allowed to experience something with you, it becomes more special. Those will be special memories for all of us."

That's the way it is with Ryan. He's a family man who seems more comfortable doing things for others than being on the receiving end himself. Ryan once gave the Astros' bullpen catcher a new shotgun. That was akin to Dan Marino, the Miami Dolphins' quarterback, presenting his offensive linemen gloves at Christmas after Marino set a pro football record for touchdown passes.

Frequently, Ryan's gifts are more personal, like the time two years ago when he called up a friend and said he needed some help.

"I asked him what he needed," said Larry Phillips, a ranching friend. "He said, 'I've just got to come over.' I told him I had to be home by 7:30, and he said that would be enough time. He came over, and we went down to the county fair. We looked around, then we went back home. My yard was full of cars. He and my wife had pulled a surprise (birthday) party on me."

Outfielder Jose Cruz spent seven years alongside Ryan with the Astros before announcing his retirement at the end of a subpar season. Ryan admired the way Cruz played the game, and worried that his contributions would go unrecognized.

One day he approached reporters from two Houston papers and handed them three sheets of paper filled with his best longhand. It was a column he had written to tell Cruz thanks. Said Ryan, "I'd like you to run it if you could."

With the Cruz column in mind, *Houston Post* sports editor Ivy McLemore called Ryan before the 5,000-strikeout game last August. He asked Ryan if he would write a first-person column about his strikeouts, and Ryan instinctively consented.

The *Post* fax machine hummed with six handwritten pages sent by Ryan a day before the start. "We changed only two words," McLemore said. "It was meticulous."

Ryan adjusts his ice pack while talking with the media after his 300th win.

There's a part of Ryan in Ewell's backyard rock garden. "I pick up rocks wherever I am and bring them home. I've got 'em from Stone Mountain, I've got some that were in an earthquake in Los Angeles," the trainer said. "I asked Nolan, 'When you go out to the ranch some time, could you bring me back some pretty stones?' He came in the next day with five or six beautiful stones."

Ryan may have as many friends outside baseball as within.

"I'm just a poor, dumb country boy," said Phillips. "But I could call Nolan in the middle of the night and he would do anything."

President George Bush called Ryan on New Year's Day last year with a last-minute opening in a golf foursome. Ryan considers Bush a friend, but declined that invitation.

"Now, if he had called me when he was going hunting, that might have been different," Ryan said, "but we had plans with the family."

Ryan has been around long enough that five of his former teammates now manage in the major leagues: Bud Harrelson, Art Howe, Frank Robinson, Jeff Torborg and Bobby Valentine. He has shared clubhouse space with Tom Seaver, Rod Carew, Don Baylor and Mike Scott, to name a few perennial All-Stars. Yet he seems drawn more to the people on baseball's fringe, people who do not think they are a big deal.

His best friends with the Astros were middle reliever Danny Darwin and Harry Spilman, a career .237 hitter who loves the game enough to still be playing for Tucson (Pacific Coast) at age 36. Oliver, who played nine years and got into only seven major league games, has become Ryan's best buddy with the Rangers.

They had never met before the spring of 1989, but vacationed together last December at the National Finals Rodeo in Las Vegas. Oliver, a Californian, went there wearing boots he had bought with a gift certificate Ryan received for appearing on a post-game show.

Abilene (Texas) native Bill Gilbreth appeared in 14 games as a major league pitcher. Three of those were during an abbreviated stint with the California Angels in 1974. Ryan was a teammate. "He was becoming a superstar," Gilbreth said, "and I wasn't even becoming."

Ryan and Gilbreth have stayed in touch through the years. The friendship culminated with the Ryan name building a baseball program from scratch at Abilene Christian University. Theirs is the typical Ryan relationship.

"I'm about as plain as you can get," said Gilbreth, who became an accountant after his baseball career. "I know what I am, and I know who he is. But we were brought up alike. It doesn't matter how much money a person has. It's what he wants to be. I guess that's why my family has always liked him a lot. He is a genuine person. He's never forgotten his roots as a small-town person from Texas."

Phillips, 52, joins veterinarian Beryl Kleine and banker Stacy Botter on the inner circle of Ryan's friends in Alvin. Phillips actually lives a few miles away in the small town of Manvel. He knew of Ryan, but didn't meet him until 1979.

They have become hunting buddies and unpaid laborers on each other's projects. Ryan and Phillips loan tractors and other farm equipment back and forth like housewives once swapped recipes over the back fence, and Ryan's children can often be found fishing at a lake behind Phillips' house. Ruth Ryan, Nolan's wife, sometimes helps Phillips haul hay.

When Ryan wanted to get away from the pressure that came with his decision to leave the Astros two years ago, he and Phillips retreated to Ryan's ranch in Cotulla, Texas.

"He said, 'Larry, come with me, I've got to get away for a few days,'" Phillips said. "We stayed there five days, and didn't go anywhere. No TV, no newspaper, nothing. He just wanted to think things out."

To become a Ryan intimate is an unexpected thrill for Phillips, who only goes to one or two Astros games a year. "Here's this guy who has all the records, has done all this stuff, and here I am, a dumb old country boy," he said. "I wondered what he was doing with me. But after I got to know him, he was as comfortable to be around as your own brother."

When Larry and Nancy Phillips celebrated their 25th wedding anniversary, the Ryans sent flowers to the house. Ruth, driving her Mercedes for the occasion, then picked up the celebrating couple and took them to the Astrodome for a game. They had dinner in the stadium club, and saw their names on the scoreboard: "Congratulations, Larry and Nancy Phillips."

"He leaned out of the dugout, looked up where we were sitting and kind of smiled," Phillips said. "He didn't have to do that."

Ryan helped Phillips cope with the back-to-back deaths of his parents a few years ago. "He would call me night and day," Phillips said. The caring was returned last winter, when Ryan's mother died. Phillips also helped Ryan wrestle with the difficult decision to sell off many of his best cattle last spring.

Ryan had lovingly built up a herd of purebred stock, looking forward to the day when he could oversee it on a full-time basis.

He had too little time to devote to the herd, and government regulations made it too much work for too little profit. He forced himself to sell stock worth almost $500,000 early this year.

"Nolan had worked long and hard to get the cattle together, and now he was selling them," said

300-VICTORY CLUB		
1.	Cy Young	511
2.	Walter Johnson	416
3.	Christy Mathewson	373
	Grover Alexander	373
5.	Warren Spahn	363
6.	Pud Galvin	361
7.	Kid Nichols	360
8.	Tim Keefe	344
9.	Steve Carlton	329
10.	John Clarkson	328
11.	Eddie Plank	327
12.	Don Sutton	324
13.	Phil Niekro	318
14.	Gaylord Perry	314
15.	Mickey Welch	311
	Tom Seaver	311
17.	Old Hoss Radbourn	308
18.	Lefty Grove	300
	Early Wynn	300
	Nolan Ryan	**300**

Phillips, who accompanied Ryan to the sale. "We went downstairs for breakfast at the hotel, and he just kept sitting there. I could tell he was in no hurry to sell his cattle. I put my arm around him, and told him he sure was a sad sight."

Ryan had a similar expression on his face when animal-control officers once had to destroy two coyote pups Ryan had brought back to his house after a ride into the country. One of the coyotes bit Ryan, which stopped being funny when the threat of rabies was mentioned.

There were two choices: Put Ryan through the series of rabies shots, which probably would have meant missing a start or two with the Astros, or test the pups. They could only be tested after they had been killed.

"He was willing to take the shots, but somebody convinced him that the shots were long and painful, and there were more coyotes out there," Phillips said. "There are two things he won't do. One is all that trash on the highways. You couldn't hold a gun to his head and make him throw something out his car window. The other is hurt an animal. He sees anything hurt or crippled, and he's going to do everything he can to help it get better."

> **"I have the utmost respect for him, more as a person than a baseball player," Gilbreth said. "That's saying a lot. He's done things in baseball that won't be surpassed."**

The one time Ryan won't satisfy an autograph seeker is when he is eating in a restaurant. Phillips laughs about a time he and Ryan were eating in a barbecue restaurant in Houston.

"We had been at a cattle sale, and people had been bugging Nolan all day," Phillips said. "We go to this restaurant that's got good barbecue and great onion rings. We're sitting there eating, and this table full of girls just starts looking at us. Then one of 'em can't take it any longer. She gets up and comes over to our table with a camera.

"She says, 'I'm sorry to bother you, but we're from New York and I've never seen onion rings as big as those. Do you mind if I take a picture of the onion rings?' They didn't know Nolan from Joe Blow. I said, 'You should have held them up so when the pictures were developed somebody would say, "Hey isn't that Nolan Ryan with the onion rings?"' It was great to see him get shot down by onion rings."

Ryan's name recognition has turned into a national calling card. While he has become a paid spokesmen for products that range from Advil to Whataburger and Wrangler jeans, he devotes more time to charities. He's a sucker for a good cause.

He lost his father to lung cancer in 1970, and since then has worked to raise money for cancer research. He does public service announcements for the American Cancer Society and speaks out against smokeless tobacco with an organization called Athletes Through With Chew. He will be a keynote speaker at a September luncheon to support the M.D. Anderson Cancer Center in Houston.

Ryan's annual round of golf comes in the Nolan Ryan Golf Classic, which raises funds for Alvin Community College, where he attended some classes and was awarded an honorary degree. He is also a spokesman for Special Olympics, the Texas Shriners' Hospital, a national physical-education program and a rodeo cowboy crisis fund. He participated in Little League's 50th anniversary last year.

Through Gilbreth, briefly his teammate in California, Ryan raised $258,000 to start a baseball program at Abilene Christian.

"I have the utmost respect for him, more as a person than a baseball player," Gilbreth said. "That's saying a lot. He's done things in baseball that won't be surpassed."

Pass the fried pies.

MAN OF THE YEAR

by DAVE NIGHTINGALE   **JANUARY 7, 1991**

ARLINGTON—Whether it's a blessing or a curse, only the athlete himself can tell you. But it is almost impossible to address the subject of Nolan Ryan without using numbers, lots of 'em.

The basic Ryan digits, though, are as simple as one, two, three. Strike one! Strike two! Strike three, and take a hike!

Not only does Ryan hold baseball's all-time strikeout record (5,308), his total is 28 percent higher than that of second-place Steve Carlton—a margin that will continue to grow because Ryan's career isn't over.

But there's one number in the Ryan resume that has to be a little galling. That number comes up when one asks how many times Ryan has won the Cy Young Award over the last 23 seasons. The answer is zero.

The Cy Young is supposed to be the hallmark for a pitcher, and Ryan is a hallmark unto himself, a man who has pitched six no-hitters (two more than anybody else), a man who has struck out 9.57 batters for every nine innings he has worked since 1967, a man who has started 706 games (the fifth highest total in history) and has pitched 4,990⅓ innings, a man who is one of only 20 pitchers to win 300 games in his career.

It may be argued by some curmudgeons that Ryan was chosen Man of the Year on the basis of an entire career, not for his actions of the last 12 months. And it is true that you can't entirely divorce the past when you consider the talents of the Aged Aquarian (Ryan will turn 44 on January 31), the oldest player in the major leagues.

So, what did make Ryan something extra special in 1990, beyond the fact that he posted a 13-9 mark for the Texas Rangers, a team that had only a .500 record in the 140 decisions in which Ryan was not involved?

The answer probably has something to do with one or all of the following:

• On June 11, Ryan pitched the sixth hitless game of his career, becoming the only man to accomplish the no-hit feat in each of three different decades. He faced only 29 batters, striking out 14 of them. He threw the ball five mph faster in the last two innings than during the first seven. His victims were the defending world champion Oakland Athletics, not some second-division rinky-dinks.

• The no-hitter came less than a week after he had come off the disabled list (he had suffered muscle spasms in his back). Two days after the no-hitter, doctors determined that he had pitched the milestone contest with a stress fracture of vertebrae in his lower back. "Aw, shoot, it wasn't all that bad," Ryan said. "It only hurt when I threw the ball. I felt all right the rest of the time."

• On April 26, Ryan pitched a one-hit, 1-0 victory over the Chicago White Sox, a team that would win 94 games in 1990. The hit was a second-inning single by Ron Kittle. The one-hitter was the 12th of Ryan's career, enabling him to tie Bob Feller for the major league record in that category.

• On July 31, he beat the Milwaukee Brewers, 11-3, for his 300th victory. He finished the season with 302 career victories, 18th on the all-time list. "That's an accomplishment worth remembering, because nobody's going to win 300 anymore," Detroit Tigers manager Sparky Anderson insisted. Only the California Angels' Bert Blyleven—who has 279 victories and who will be 40 years old when the 1991 season opens—is in a position to argue the point.

• Even though the aging process reduced Ryan's fastball to a mere 95 mph, he still led all American League pitchers in strikeouts last year with 232. His average of 10.43 strikeouts per nine innings pitched in 1990 was nearly a full strikeout above his career average. And in 1973, when he set a modern single-season strikeout record (383) as a 26-year-old, his strikeout average per nine innings was just 10.57.

• In 1990, American League hitters had a composite batting average of only .188 against Ryan. That was 28 points less than the average against league runner-up Randy Johnson of Seattle and 40 points below the average allowed by some guy in Boston named Roger Clemens. Sid Fernandez of the New York Mets was the National League leader, allowing an average of .200.

Beyond pure progress and performance, there are a lot of intangibles that go into the selection of TSN's Man of the Year.

The sports year in 1990 was filled with many unpleasant odors.

Perched above this morass was Ryan, a quiet, soft-talking "good ol' boy" from Texas who is more at home behind the wheel of a 4x4 than a Lamborghini, a family man, a generous contributor to the welfare of the planet, a role model for every mother's son.

This is the Ryan who once accepted a free-agent contract from the Houston Astros when more money was available elsewhere so that he could spend more time at his ranch, 20 miles away in Alvin (Texas), while his three children, Reese, Reid and Wendy, were still in the formative years.

This is the Ryan who sat next to 14-year-old Reese on the Rangers' bench last June 11, laughing inwardly as the teenager gave him pep talks and back rubs while trying to relax his father's mind and the muscles that were in the process of pitching a no-hitter.

This is the Ryan who pours time, energy and money into raising funds to provide college scholarships, medical benefits for rodeo cowboys who can't buy insurance and new facilities for children's hospitals in the Dallas and Houston areas.

He may not be the hippest and handsomest dude on the prairie. And only his wife, Ruth, or members of the hairpiece industry might be inter-

The Sporting News

ested in running their fingers across his balding scalp.

But to *The Sporting News*, Ryan seemed like a breath of fresh air in 1990—while much of the rest of the world seemed to be going slightly mad.

On a recent winter day, Ryan sprawled in front of his dressing cubicle in the Rangers' locker room at Arlington Stadium, where he had gone for a workout, and expounded on some of the highlights and lowlights of his career. Obviously, he couldn't expound on all of them, simply because there wasn't enough time.

"It's kind of difficult to rank what I consider my top achievements," Ryan said, "because each of them has represented some different aspect of my career.

"The 5,000 strikeouts? That's a tribute to my longevity and durability. It shows I've been able to maintain a certain style of pitching for a long period of time.

"The 300 victories? That showed my consistency and it put me on a level with a lot of great pitchers. But it also was very, very satisfying because I never anticipated I'd be able to do it. Remember, I played with a lot of clubs (the Mets of the late 1960s, the Angels of the 1970s, the Astros of the 1980s) that had a lot of trouble scoring. I didn't even consider I could reach the 300 level until I got to about 200.

"The six no-hitters? They reflect the fact I was able to maintain my good stuff over a long period of time. Actually, they were a lot more exciting on a personal basis because they took place over 18 years and because of the element of surprise. You're aware of your career totals. You can observe your progress in improving them. But a no-hitter is an unsuspecting event that just happens."

Ryan should reach another plateau, 5,000 innings pitched, sometime in April. He was asked if he would consider that achievement on a par with the others.

Ryan looked puzzled. "Haven't I pitched 5,000 innings yet?" he asked.

Told that he was 9⅓ innings shy of that total, Ryan said, "Oh, I didn't know that."

And you thought this guy was hung up on his numbers?

Ryan clearly enjoys his role as baseball's senior statesman, now that he has made certain adjustments.

"As I get older, I have a much better perspective," he said. "I have more knowledge of pitching and conditioning; I have greater self-confidence.

"I love baseball now for different reasons—for the need to stay in shape, for the competition, for the camaraderie with my teammates, even though most of them view me more as a coach than a teammate. I don't enjoy the trips like I did when I was younger. It was exciting to travel back then. I had a different point of view. But I felt a lot more pressure back then, too."

The pitcher is acutely aware that Von Ryan's Express is about to pull into the station for the last time.

"I hate to say it, but developing a back problem, like I did last season, usually means that the end is near," Ryan said.

Ryan has no doubts about his ability to perform well in 1991. But he can't begin to prove that he will, not yet.

"I feel real good, in general," he said, "but I don't know if it will hurt me to throw because I have not thrown a ball since the season ended."

And when he does retire?

"Well, I'm looking forward to the free time, but I also know that I'll miss the excitement and the attention," he said.

As long as he has a name-recognition factor—which, in Texas might continue for a long time—he'll probably continue with his charitable fund-raising and with his television commercial endorsements (for such commodities as jeans, boots, shavers, airlines and headache pills).

One thing he might do with his free time is put together a herd of purebred cattle once again. "Right now, I run my entire ranch as a producer of commercial beef," he said. "I had a purebred herd once before, but I had to sell it off because I didn't have the time to devote to it."

Or, he might consider a career in Texas politics, although the job that interests him the most currently is occupied by a friend.

Ryan will not become a sportswriter—even though he has penned guest columns for Houston newspapers on a few occasions. He said that writing those articles, in longhand, was both time-consuming and agonizing.

"It is hard to consider the future after baseball," Ryan conceded. "The game has dominated my life and I'll sure miss it when I have to leave it. There will be adjustments to be made, both monetarily and emotionally. How easy or how tough that will be, I just don't know."

A DAY WHEN CRASS GAVE WAY TO CLASS

MAY 13, 1991

Their paths had crossed on big days before, these two future Hall of Famers. On August 22, 1989, the day Nolan Ryan registered his 5,000th strikeout, Rickey Henderson was there. In fact, Henderson was victim No. 5,000.

And last June 11, when Ryan pitched his sixth career no-hitter, Oakland's Henderson made the final out. The next day, against Ryan's Texas team, Henderson reached a milestone of his own with his 900th stolen base.

This time, they were some 1,700 miles apart when baseball's spotlight shined on one and then, several hours later, the other. Henderson was the first to make history last Wednesday.

In the fourth inning, on a 1-and-0 pitch from Tim Leary of the Yankees to Athletics designated hitter Harold Baines, Henderson did what he does best. He bolted off second base and slid headfirst into third, beating the throw from catcher Matt Nokes. It was stolen base No. 939, a major league record, surpassing the mark set by Lou Brock.

Let's go to the videotape.

Henderson jumps to his feet, yanks the base out of the ground and holds it high above his head. He pumps his fist and waves to the crowd. The game comes to a halt while Henderson's mother, Bobbie, and Brock come out of the stands. Henderson accepts congratulations from the man he has just replaced as baseball's stolen-base king, then grabs the microphone.

"Lou Brock was a symbol of great basestealing," he says. "But today, I am the greatest of all time."

Later that night in Arlington, Texas...

There are two outs in the top of the ninth as Ryan stands on the mound and faces Toronto's Roberto Alomar. The count is 2-and-2. Ryan takes a deep breath, winds and delivers.

Strike three. Ryan's 16th strikeout of the game and the exclamation point to the seventh no-hitter of his career.

A tip of his hat, a big, toothy grin and the 44-year-old righthander is mobbed by his teammates. After the game, Ryan discusses his latest feat.

"It was the most rewarding no-hitter of them all because it came in front of my fans on Arlington Appreciation Night," he says. "My career is complete now. I got one for the fans in Arlington."

No reference about being the greatest ever. Nothing about how he pitched like a superstar. Just a comment about how happy he was to have done it for the home crowd.

Too bad Henderson couldn't have handled his moment of renown with similar decorum. He may have surpassed Brock in stolen bases and beaten Ryan to the spotlight, but he's miles behind both in grace and humility.

Interestingly, the "greatest of all time" victimized more than 300 major league pitchers—from Jim Abbott to Geoff Zahn—en route to his basestealing mark. But not one of those 939 thefts came with Ryan on the mound.

The significance of that fact is diminished only because during most of Henderson's major league career, Ryan pitched in the National League. Only in Henderson's rookie season, 1979, and the last three years have they had the opportunity to face each other.

Still, we think that's some measure of poetic justice, particularly in light of each man's deportment last Wednesday. It was a day when Henderson and Ryan displayed two forms of speed, but only one man exhibited class.

Ryan achieved his seventh career no-hitter on May 1, 1991, against the Toronto Blue Jays.

May 1, 1991
Texas 3, Toronto 0

TORONTO	ab	r	h	bi
White cf	4	0	0	0
R. Alomar 2b	4	0	0	0
Gruber 3b	2	0	0	0
Carter lf	2	0	0	0
Olerud 1b	3	0	0	0
Whiten rf	3	0	0	0
G. Hill dh	3	0	0	0
Myers c	3	0	0	0
M. Lee ss	3	0	0	0
TOTALS	27	0	0	0

TEXAS	ab	r	h	bi
Pettis cf	4	1	1	0
Daugherty lf	4	0	1	0
Palmeiro 1b	4	1	2	0
Sierra rf	4	1	1	2
Franco 2b	4	0	0	0
Gonzalez dh	3	0	1	0
Stanley c	3	0	1	0
Buechele 3b	4	0	1	0
Huson ss	2	0	0	0
	32	3	8	2

Toronto	0 0 0	0 0 0	0 0 0—0
Texas	0 0 3	0 0 0	0 0 x—3

E—Gruber, Myers, M. Lee, Palmeiro. LOB—Toronto 2, Texas 8. 2B—Gonzalez, Stanley. HR—Sierra. SB—Pettis. CS—Gonzalez. S—Huson.

TORONTO	IP	H	R	ER	BB	SO
Key (L 4-1)	6	5	3	3	1	5
MacDonald	1	2	0	0	0	2
Fraser	1	1	0	0	0	0

TEXAS						
Ryan (W 3-2)	9	0	0	0	2	16

HBP—by Fraser (Gonzalez).

AP/Wide World Photos

Q & A WITH NOLAN RYAN

The Rangers' Nolan Ryan capped a magical day in baseball history last Wednesday with his seventh career no-hitter. At 44, the game's ageless wonder struck out 16 Blue Jay hitters and displayed a 96-mph fastball. And he's not done yet.

Q: How does this no-hitter differ from your other six?

A: This one is a reflection of me as a more complete pitcher. I got by on raw physical ability in some of the first ones. I'm a better pitcher now. I don't have as much raw ability as I had 15 or 20 years ago, but I compensate with better control and better command.

Q: Much has been made about your conditioning program. For instance, you were in the clubhouse lifting weights early in the morning after your no-hitter. Where do you get your work ethic?

A: I think a lot of that comes from my father. He worked two jobs (as an oil company administrator and a newspaper delivery man) to put four girls through college. I know he didn't want to get up at 1 every morning to throw the newspapers, but that's what he had to do. I think that's the way I am.

Q: The Rangers are reportedly prepared to offer you $5 million to re-sign for the 1992 season. Would you accept such a deal?

A: If the Rangers came to me, I'd probably sign. But that doesn't mean I'd play next year. If I get to the point where I'm physically unable to perform to my capabilities, to the point where I'm not effective, it will be time to retire. I'll decide that at the end of the season, as I've done the last few years.

Q: You've pitched for the Mets, Angels, Astros and Rangers. Which team's uniform will you wear when they make your likeness for the Hall of Fame?

A: I haven't been giving any thought to that. I think before I give that any thought I have to get there.

Q: With seven no-hitters and more than 300 victories and 5,000 strikeouts to your credit, what are your goals for the rest of this season?

A: I just want to stay healthy, pitch every fifth day. If I don't pitch 225 innings, I'll be disappointed. I'm really not worried about how many games I win. I want this team to do well. I would trade more individual accomplishments to have this team in the World Series.

Q: Where do your seven no-hitters and strikeout records place you in baseball history?

A: I never think about things like that. My attitude is that I'm still an active player. I don't sit around and reflect on what's happened when a game is over. I prepare myself for my next start. I have to do that so I will be ready.

OLDEST NO-HIT PITCHERS

Pitcher	Date	Age
Nolan Ryan	May 1, 1991	44 (3 months, 1 day)
Nolan Ryan	June 11, 1990	43 (4 months, 11 days)
Cy Young	June 30, 1908	41 (3 months, 1 day)
Warren Spahn	April 28, 1961	40 (5 days)
Sal Maglie	September 25, 1956	39 (4 months, 30 days)
Warren Spahn	September 16, 1960	39 (4 months, 24 days)
Cy Young	*May 5, 1904	37 (1 month, 6 days)
Bob Keegan	August 20, 1957	37 (16 days)
Allie Reynolds	September 28, 1951	36 (7 months, 18 days)
Allie Reynolds	July 12, 1951	36 (5 months, 2 days)
Bob Gibson	August 14, 1971	35 (9 months, 5 days)
Hoyt Wilhelm	September 20, 1958	35 (1 month, 25 days)

*—Perfect game

The Sporting News

"WE WON'T BACK DOWN"

by MICHAEL KNISLEY　　**AUGUST 16, 1993**

Out in California, where their Kansas City Royals were losing a series to the Angels, the McRaes, Hal and Brian, watched the interminable replays of last week's Texas Cage Match between Nolan Ryan and Robin Ventura and silently braced themselves.

It was Wednesday, August 4, which now stands as the ceremonial start to baseball's dog days, made all the more official by a nationally-distributed photograph of the Rangers-White Sox brawl that appeared to show Texas catcher Geno Petralli bulldog-biting Chicago's Bo Jackson on the wrist.

Life in the American League West is not going to be a Sunday stroll in the park between now and October 3.

"It's that time of the year," says Brian McRae, the Royals' center fielder. "It's August, and it's a pennant race. Things are going to happen. People are irritable. Tempers flare. There are things you can tolerate early in the season that you can't let happen now. People have short fuses."

Last Thursday, the day after the Ventura-Ryan brouhaha, Texas and Kevin Brown beat Chicago, 7-1, without further hostilities—which maybe isn't so surprising. If the White Sox feel the need for further reprisals, they'll want the battleground closer to home the next time.

In the days immediately following the fight, the Rangers seemed to be able to channel the adrenaline spawned by the Arlington Stadium melee into a quick three-game winning streak, while Chicago went stale in the same stretch, losing the brawl game, 5-2, after leading, 2-0, and then dropping the 7-1 decision to Brown and the series opener at home to the Angels, 7-3, last Friday night. Jack McDowell stopped the bleeding for the White Sox

with his 18th victory Saturday night, but Chicago fell to the Angels again on Sunday.

"I think it could have made a difference for the Rangers because they were at home when it happened," says Oakland's Mark McGwire, who was as fascinated by Ventura's charge toward the 46-year-old Ryan, one of the game's most hallowed institu-

AP/Wide World Photos

tions, as the rest of the baseball world was. ("It's like charging Elvis," Reds pitcher Kevin Wickander says.)

"If they're in Chicago," McGwire continues, "it might have been a different situation. When you're at home, you've got the fans on your side. They don't see what the White Sox were seeing."

The American League will step into the breach, probably this week, and could play a significant role in the division race, especially if it metes out harsher punishment to Ventura, who was ejected for charging the mound, than it does to Ryan, who was allowed to stay in the game despite getting in six good licks to the head—Ventura calls them "noogies"—to Ventura's none in Round One last week.

The White Sox are preparing for the worst.

"What's going to happen is that I'm going to be the one suspended, and he won't," Ventura says. "There is a lot of injustice going around. A couple of years ago, Jack McDowell stood there on the mound and Mark Whiten came out and decked him, and Jack got ejected, suspended and fined. (A.L. officials) can do whatever they want. There are no guidelines. Whatever they feel like."

Ryan insists he wasn't throwing at Ventura, and maybe he wasn't. But accepting his version in this case is a little like accepting the versions of the other participants, all of whom claimed to be on the infield only as peacemakers. As usual, it was next to impossible to find anyone owning up to actual fisticuffs, although when Chicago second baseman Joe Cora executed a picture-perfect Greg Louganis swan dive into the pile on the pitcher's mound, he didn't appear to have détente on his mind.

Even Mickey Hatcher, the Rangers' first-base coach, couldn't—or wouldn't—identify the perpetrator of the gash around his eye that needed three stitches to close.

If Texas was able to use the brawl to any positive purpose, it was because Ryan was still on the mound when play resumed in the third inning. He was untouchable through the next four innings, allowing only Cora to reach base on a walk before he gave way to Craig Lefferts in the eighth.

"I guess after pitching for as long as I have, you realize you still have a job to do," Ryan says. "You can't let something like that be a distraction. Maybe that's harder to do in that kind of situation than it is after a bad play or a bad call or a bad pitch, but you still have to do it. You have to overcome those things. Sometimes, an incident like that will just wake up people's intensity—put them on a little higher level. It wakes up their competitive juices."

The carryover Kennedy wanted out of the fracas came in Brown's performance the next night ($7^2/_3$ innings, 6 hits, 1 run), in Kenny Rogers' outing against Seattle on Friday night (7 innings, 5 hits, 3 runs in a 5-3 victory), in Roger Pavlik's 13-strikeout, nine-inning 2-1 loss to Seattle on Saturday and in Steve Dreyer's five shutout innings of Sunday's 7-1 victory over the Mariners.

Until Ryan emerged from the post-fight wreckage to baffle the White Sox last Wednesday, the Rangers' starting pitchers had been 6-9 with a 6.35 ERA since the All-Star break, and the staff as a whole ranked 13th in the league at 5.55 since July 13. Its ERA was higher than any other major-league team playing .500 or better baseball. Even at 22-14 in its last 36 games, Texas wasn't pitching effectively, with a 5.06 ERA over that stretch.

"That's why I wanted to talk more about Nolan's pitching performance than anything else that happened," Kennedy says. "That's the presence we need, somebody like that to go out there and throw strikes and be aggressive with his stuff against good hitters and not have any fear. Go after people. When Nolan was out there, you saw a veteran go out and take charge of the game. I'm not specifically talking about the incident, although that's part of it. But it's the veteran presence I've been talking about. Maybe that'll rub off on some of these younger pitchers."

The brawl certainly will be a benchmark for the 1993 season, the last of Ryan's 27 big league years, regardless of whether it has lasting effects on the division race. But if the Rangers stay hot and the White Sox stay sluggish, last Wednesday night will be the turning point.

> **"Sometimes, an incident like that will just wake up people's intensity—put them on a little higher level. It wakes up their competitive juices."**
> **—Nolan Ryan**

Arlington Stadium draws a crowd on Nolan Ryan Day, September 12, 1993.

Ryan receives a standing ovation from both fans and teammates.

Ryan addresses the crowd on Nolan Ryan Day.

CHAPTER 9

INTO THE SUNSET

NOLAN RYAN

T he standards set by Nolan Ryan in a career that began three decades ago will stand tall for the ages. Ryan is a legend. A hero. A future Hall of Famer. And after 27 seasons, 324 victories, seven no-hitters and 5,714 strikeouts, it is finally time for Alvin, Texas' most famous rancher to ride off into the sunset.

It ended 9,884 days after it started on September 11, 1966. The last 181 of those days—the 1993 major league baseball regular season—are the longest and most painful. It maybe isn't surprising that Nolan Ryan comes to this realization in the visiting- team clubhouse at Fenway Park in August.

"My style of pitching seems to have been lost somewhere in baseball," Ryan says in Boston. "I mean, it's antiquated now. It's just another reason why I feel like it's time for me to get out, because I'm not going to change. I have to do what I think is right."

Michael Knisley, The Sporting News

I just keep 'em high, inside & fast.

27 seasons worth of strikes.

Louis DeLuca

THE END

by MICHAEL KNISLEY   **SEPTEMBER 22, 1993**

SEATTLE—There is a nice symmetry to it. Nolan Ryan's last pitch in the major leagues is a fastball. To Dave Magadan, the seventh hitter in the first inning of his last game in the big leagues, Ryan throws a fastball.

"I felt the pop in my elbow, and then I had a real bad burning sensation and muscle spasms," he says. "I guess if you're going to injure yourself and finish your career, that was the way to do it—throwing my bread-and-butter pitch, the pitch that was the basis for everything I accomplished."

The recovery time from surgery to repair a torn ulnar collateral ligament in a pitching elbow generally is at least a year. Ryan has 11 days to recover, so he knows immediately.

"There's no way I'll ever pitch again," he says.

On the mound, he speaks briefly with Danny Wheat, the trainer, and simply walks to the dugout, in much the same manner he walks away with the rib-cage injury in August.

"My heart fell," Kennedy says. "It just sunk. It's the first time I've felt like that for a player in a long time. I just felt bad for him, to have to go out that way. Of all things, for the arm to finally blow out."

Twenty-seven years after he breaks into the majors in a relief role for the Mets on September 11, 1966, this is the pitching line for Ryan's last appearance: Zero innings, two hits, five runs, five earned runs, four walks, no strikeouts.

"Ending my career this way, the pennant race, the

bad outing contributing to another loss, not even being able to get through the first inning—all those things are depressing," he says.

Depressing and unfortunate. But does he deserve this? The "Tank McNamara" strip a week later is a farewell ceremony in a baseball stadium. Tank, the ex-jock turned broadcaster, covers the festivities this way: "Number 34 is special because it was the number of the immortal Biff 'The Stiff' Duper. The Bashers are retiring it...because no one else will wear it." The illustration is of a fat, balding, sorry jock waving to the crowd. No. 34. Ryan's number.

The Sporting News

THE LAST TIME

by MICHAEL KNISLEY　　　　**OCTOBER 3, 1993**

ARLINGTON—The confluences of baseball bring the Kansas City Royals to Texas today, so the game can say goodbye to Nolan Ryan, George Brett and Arlington Stadium all at once. Fittingly, Ryan and Brett present the lineup cards to the umpiring crew before the game.

Ryan is in his uniform for the first time since Seattle and for the final time as a player. After the game, he is feted as a member of the Rangers' all-time team, as voted by the fans.

Officially now, he is a private citizen.

"I'm going into what I call my normal offseason activities," he says. "I don't think the adjustment is going to really take place until next spring, when everybody else starts getting ready to go to spring training and I'm sitting around."

Ryan isn't finished with baseball. He has a 10-year personal services contract with the Rangers that will keep him occupied with the game in some as yet to be determined capacity. He isn't leaving us entirely.

So it's altogether fitting and proper, maybe, that as he ends his final news conference in the Rangers' clubhouse late this afternoon, he walks away from the crowd of reporters, stops and asks, "Hey what's happening in the Dodgers-Giants game?"

AP/Wide World Photos

NOLAN IN THE NEWS

Nolan Ryan's long, distinguished career has been chronicled in many forms. Here we take a look at how *The Sporting News* covered Ryan at different points along the way.

April 30, 1966

The windup: The first reference to Nolan Ryan in TSN

The pitch: "Sharp pitching at the proper time helped the trio of winners in opening games of the Western Carolinas League on April 18. The fourth contest ended in a 5-5 tie, called at the end of 13 innings due to curfew.

"Righthander Nolan Ryan pitched the only complete game of the first-nighters, hurling the Greenville Mets to a 6-3 win over the host Spartanburg Phillies, allowing six scattered singles and fanning 14. Mike Mitchell homered for the Mets."

May 28, 1966

The windup: The headline—Ryan Racing to Flashy Start As Met Greenie in Greenville

The pitch: "...Nolan Ryan is in his first full season of organized ball, wears the uniform of the Greenville Mets and ranks as one of the parent New York club's top mound prospects.

"He started the Western Carolinas League season by tossing 25 scoreless innings and, in six games, compiled 62 strikeouts and a 4-0 record."

October 9, 1971

The windup: Mets Swap Ryan? "No Way," Says Gil

The pitch: "Any speculation that the Mets were about ready to give up on Nolan Ryan were quickly dismissed by manager Gil Hodges even before the hard-throwing righthander ended a seven-week drought with a victory over the Cubs.

"'Oh, no,' said the manager, suggesting genuine surprise that anyone would even entertain such a thought. 'We never have given any consideration to trading Nolan Ryan.'"

May 5, 1973

The windup: Angels Growing Plump on Ryan's K Rations

The pitch: "'It's unfair,' said Hisle with a trace of a smile. 'When I was in the National League, we never swung at Ryan's curveball. We knew it wasn't going to be over the plate. It's not fair for any pitcher to have a curve like Ryan's, not if he has *that* fastball.'

"Indeed, the Ryan Express opened the season highballing down the road to Cooperstown. He won his first three starts in impressive fashion. The man who led the majors in strikeouts (329) and tied for the lead in shutouts (9) last season fanned 12, 11 and 14.

"...Like most emerging superstars, the fans want to know what Lynn Nolan Ryan, Jr. is like. These phrases fit: always friendly, down to earth, unpretentious, unassuming, unemotional."

June 2, 1973

The windup: (No-hitter No. 1) Ryan's No-No Spikes Royals' Protest

The pitch: "Nolan Ryan thanked catcher Jeff Torborg, shortstop Rudy Meoli and outfielder Ken Berry, along with muscleman Bob Oliver, for their parts in his 3-0 no-hitter at Kansas City May 15.

"But he also was ready to thank Jack McKeon, the manager of the Royals. McKeon played the game under protest and tried to upset the Angels' pitcher with appeals he was pitching illegally.

"'I want to thank Jack,' Ryan said the day after striking out 12 and walking three. 'Jack did me a favor causing all that commotion. When I bring my foot off the rubber (the basis of McKeon's appeal), it usually means that I'm rocking back too far and I get wild, high.

"'He didn't shake me up, he settled me down. I cut my back stride and everything turned out just fine.'"

July 28, 1973

The windup: (No-hitter No. 2) Ryan's Smoke

Sends Tigers into No-Hit Blind

The pitch: "...Exactly two months after the righthander shut out the Royals at Kansas City, Ryan became the fifth pitcher in major league history to record two no-hitters in a single season.

"He struck out 17 at Tiger Stadium while walking four..."

August 31, 1974

The windup: 19 Whiffs ... Some Day Ryan May Strike out 27

The pitch: "Nolan Ryan doesn't believe it is humanly possible for any major league pitcher to strike out every batter (27) in a major league game. But he may come close some day.

"All it will take is (a) a free-swinging team like Boston, Detroit or Kansas City; (b) a 100-mph fastball and (c) a more sympathetic umpire like the retired Ed Runge, whose heart was a mile wild and who had a strike zone to match.

"Reflecting back on August 12, when he fanned 19 Boston batters to equal the record for a nine-inning game shared by the Mets' Tom Seaver and the Phils' Steve Carlton, then with the Cardinals, Ryan thought he could have recorded two or three more strikeouts."

October 12, 1974

The windup: (No-hitter No. 3) Ryan Roars into Feller's Class with Third Gem

The pitch: "No-hitters are almost becoming routine with Ryan. He has learned to take his telephone off the hook. He doesn't become excited after performing one of the rarest feats in sports. 'I try to take it in stride,' he said simply.

" 'I felt like I might have a good game,' he admitted later. 'I warmed up well and the first pitch had good velocity.' His first seven pitches were strikes and he fanned the side in the first and second innings."

June 14, 1975

The windup: (No-hitter No. 4) Ryan's Pace: Four No-Hitters in Two-Year Span

The pitch: "The Angels' superstar tied Sandy

Koufax's record with his fourth, when he beat Baltimore, 1-0, at Anaheim Stadium on June 1.

"Ryan has thrown a no-hitter once every 27.2 starts since getting the hang of it in his first no-no against Kansas City on May 15, 1973. The most overpowering figure in the game, Ryan has fired four no-hitters in 109 starts."

October 10, 1981

The windup: (No-hitter No. 5) Coolest in Dome? No-Hit Ryan

The pitch: "Only one Astro remained completely unflappable. 'Shoot, I don't get emotional about these things anymore,' Ryan would say after becoming the first major-leaguer to pitch five no-hitters."

July 22, 1985

The windup: (Strikeout No. 4,000) Ryan Records Special K

The pitch: "Baseball's 4,000-strikeout club has its first member—Nolan Ryan."

September 4, 1989

The windup: (Strikeout No. 5,000)

The pitch: "Ryan made Oakland's Rickey Henderson victim No. 5,000 in the fifth inning August 22 before a crowd of 42,869 at Arlington Stadium. Ryan fanned Henderson with a fastball that was clocked at 96 mph on the Rangers' radar gun."

June 25, 1990

The windup: (No-Hitter No. 6) No. 6! The Rub on Ryan's No-Hitter: Could Back Pain Be a Signal That the End of a Long Career is Near?

The pitch: "Ryan, 43, extended the boundary of his legend out into baseball's stratosphere that night, using his fastball and a wicked changeup to overpower the defending world champion A's. He struck out 14 and walked two in becoming, among other things, the first major league pitcher to throw no-hitters in three decades (1970s, '80s and '90s)

"'The thing I'll get chills about wasn't the last out or any out in the ninth,' said Rangers manager Bobby Valentine. 'The scene I'll remember is Nolan on the bench with his son rubbing his back and patting him on the leg, giving him a pep talk. No

---

KING COVER

Not surprisingly, Ryan has been on the cover of The Sporting News many times over the years, 11 to be exact. You could call him TSN's cover king: Twice he was the "Fireball King," and in 1983 he graduated to "Whiff King." The Fireball King made his debut in May 1973. Long live the king.

one else could bear to talk to him. That was a wonderful sight.'"

August 13, 1990

The windup: (300th victory) Ryan's Song: Little Things Mean a Lot

The pitch: "While raw power and stubborn longevity mark Ryan as baseball's newest 300-game winner, it's little things that make the man. Little things like honesty and consideration. Little things like sincerity and generosity.

"'People who read about him in newspapers or a book tell you he can't be that good of a person,' said Dave Oliver, third-base coach of the Texas Rangers, for whom Ryan now pitches. 'But if you're around him all the time, you know that's him.'"

January 7, 1991

The windup: TSN's Man of the Year

The pitch: "...the man who has done all of this never has been deemed good enough to win the Cy Young Award. It seems ludicrous.

"Since *The Sporting News* is not into revisionist history, it can't undo any shortcomings of the past. But it certainly can decide that Lynn Nolan Ryan, Jr. is most worthy of being named to receive its prestigious Man of the Year Award. And, for 1990, TSN did just that."

May 13, 1991

The windup: (No-Hitter No. 7) A day when crass gave way to class

The pitch: "A tip of his hat, a big, toothy grin and the 44-year-old righthander is mobbed by his teammates. After the game, Ryan discusses his latest feat.

"'It was the most rewarding no-hitter of them all because it came in front of my fans on Arlington Appreciation Night,' he says. 'My career is complete now. I got one for the fans in Arlington.'"

Louis DeLuca

Ryan acknowledges the crowd in Arlington on Nolan Ryan Day in 1993.

The Sporting News

"Every hitter likes fastballs, just like everybody likes ice cream. But you don't like it when someone's stuffing it into you by the gallon. That's how you feel when Ryan's throwing balls by you. You just hope to mix in a walk so you can have a good night and only go 0-for-3."
—Reggie Jackson

10

THE LEGEND LIVES ON

NOLAN RYAN

W hile pitching in four different decades, Nolan Ryan established himself as one of the premier pitchers in baseball history. He lays claim to over 50 pitching records, many of which (including his 5,714 career strikeouts, seven no-hitters, and 383 strikeouts in a season) may stand forever. In January 1999, he was part of one of the strongest classes ever eligible for the Hall of Fame. Ryan and two other first-time nominees, George Brett and Robin Yount, were the three new members elected by the Baseball Writers' Association of America. Induction ceremonies on July 25, 1999 will honor Ryan with his well-deserved place in Cooperstown, NY, among baseball's elite performers.

Louis DeLuca

NO DEBATE: RYAN, ROSE DESERVING OF HALL

by MOSS KLEIN　　　**AUGUST 6, 1990**

Midsummer baseball thoughts usually focus on the way the division races are shaping up, but this season two of the hottest debates centered around the Hall of Fame merits of two legendary players, Pete Rose and Nolan Ryan.

Negative voices about both, especially Rose, were making themselves heard, for entirely different reasons. But each will receive this vote in his first year of eligibility.

The flawed arguments being made against Ryan are that his career won-lost record isn't Hall of Fame caliber, that he has allowed a record number of walks (40 percent more than runner-up Steve Carlton), and he has never led his league in victories or been recognized as the best pitcher in his league, as defined by the Cy Young Award.

But Ryan transcends pure numbers. He is a special-achievement pitcher, a monument to the game. Think of strikeouts, you think of Nolan Ryan. Think of no-hitters, you think of Nolan Ryan. Think of awesome power pitching, you think of Nolan Ryan. There has been no pitcher in history against whom it has been harder to get a hit, or to even hit the ball in fair territory. In terms of pure power, Ryan has been the Babe Ruth of pitchers.

For those who still want numbers, try these: Among pitchers who have worked at least 1,500 innings (Ryan is approaching 5,000), he has the lowest batting average against him, the lowest average of hits allowed per nine innings, the highest ratio of strikeouts per nine innings.

Ryan's won-lost record, in large part, is a reflection of the mediocrity of his teams—the Mets, Angels, Astros and Rangers. And while longevity itself isn't a factor, Ryan's sustained excellence over 23 years can't be ignored. He arrived in the big leagues before free agency, cable TV rights and night games in the World Series. CBS owned the Yankees, Billy Martin hadn't become a manager, Mickey Mantle was still playing, Ken Griffey, Jr. hadn't been born.

All these years and all these thousands of players later, in a baseball world barely recognizable in comparison, Ryan is still roaming the land, a dinosaur still feared, respected and admired by players barely half his age.

Louis DeLuca

ALVIN'S FAVORITE SON REACHES BASEBALL PINNACLE

by MARK BABINECK   **JANUARY 6, 1999**

ALVIN (AP) —Whether it's the Nolan Ryan Expressway leading up to nearby Houston, the bronze Nolan Ryan statue gracing city hall or the Nolan Ryan Center at the community college, a visitor gets the picture real fast.

Ryan's election Tuesday to the Baseball Hall of Fame might make him seem even larger than life now to the baseball world, but around here he's still just Nolan.

"We could have lived anywhere we wanted to," Ryan said, referring to his wife, Ruth. "But we wanted to raise our children in the same environment we were raised in."

> ## "Has the best arm I've ever seen in my life. Could be a real power pitcher some day."
> —Red Murff's scouting report on high school prospect Nolan Ryan

This town of 20,000 is used to its hometown hero making headlines, whether it's helping the New York Mets win the World Series in 1969, leading the California Angels and Houston Astros to their first division titles or putting the long-anonymous Texas Rangers on the map.

But townsfolk see beyond the record 5,714 strikeouts, seven no-hitters and dozens of other records.

"He's kind of unnoticed in a crowd," said long-time resident George Cooper, who dined with his wife, Mickey, on Tuesday at Joe's Bar-B-Q, one of the town's most popular restaurants and Ryan's personal favorite.

Mrs. Cooper added: "He's somebody for people to look up to. He's just a fine man."

Baseball's greatest power pitcher was named on 491 of the 497 ballots cast by 10-year members of the Baseball Writers' Association of America. With one more vote, he would've broken the record percentage of his former New York Mets teammate Tom Seaver.

Also elected Tuesday were George Brett and Robin Yount. It's the first time three first-time candidates have been elected since the inaugural class of 1936.

Ryan, who will sport a Rangers cap when his plaque is unveiled in Cooperstown, New York, on July 25, wears several hats these days. He's a banker, member of the state Parks and Wildlife Commission, employee of the Rangers and owner of the Astros' Class AA minor-league team.

At a news conference at Alvin Community College's Ryan Center, he said he never imagined he'd be enshrined when he signed with the New York Mets in 1965, a lanky righthander who could throw a ball as fast as he wanted, though at first he didn't always know where it was going.

"When I started out in baseball, the furthest thing from my mind was ever being in a position to be considered for the Hall of Fame," he said. "When (scout) Red Murff signed me out of high school, I had no idea if I had the ability or talent to make the big leagues."

At first he said he wanted to play four years to qualify for a pension. Then he pushed his goal to a nice, 10-year career. After signing with the Astros in

1980, becoming the first million-dollar player, at 32 he hoped he had three good years left.

When the Astros tried to cut his pay by 20 percent in 1988, he signed with Texas to play one more season so he could end his career on a high note. He played there for five years, retiring at 46 after 27 seasons in the majors.

Ryan will be the sixth former Astro in the Hall of Fame and the fifth former Ranger; none of the previous wore the hat of a Texas team on their plaque.

Ryan picked the Rangers because he felt his five years there put him over the top.

"I feel like those were very special years," said Ryan, who arguably accomplished more in Anaheim and Houston, but left both teams after neither made a serious attempt to re-sign him.

"There wasn't a lower day emotionally in my life when I signed that contract with the Rangers and came back on the plane from Atlanta and realized I was not an Astro and would no longer be an Astro," Ryan said. "When I got to Houston (in 1980), in my mind, I felt like that's where I'd end my career and had never thought any different."

He added that Angels owner Gene Autry, to whom Ryan was close, tried to lure him back to Anaheim. Ryan said it was difficult telling Autry that he wasn't going to leave Texas to play baseball again.

Rangers general manager Doug Melvin noted that the presence of virtually the entire Astros front office—none of whom were involved in his 1988 departure—was testament to Ryan's class.

"It's a great compliment to him that such a number of people are so proud of him, regardless of what hat he's wearing," Melvin said.

Ryan also noted that it was as a Ranger that he won his 300th game, struck out his 5,000th batter and tossed his sixth and seventh ho-hitters.

1999 Baseball Writers' Association of America (BBWAA) Hall of Fame Ballot Results

Player	Votes	Percentage	Player	Votes	Percentage
NOLAN RYAN	**491**	**98.79**	Bert Blyleven	70	14.08
George Brett	**488**	**98.19**	Dave Concepcion	59	11.87
Robin Yount	**385**	**77.46**	Luis Tiant	53	10.66
Carlton Fisk	330	66.40	Keith Hernandez	34	6.84
Tony Perez	302	60.76	Ron Guidry	31	6.24
Gary Carter	168	33.80	Bob Boone	27	5.43
Steve Garvey	150	30.18	Mickey Lolich*	26	5.23
Jim Rice	146	29.38	Dwight Evans	18	3.62
Bruce Sutter	121	24.35	George Bell	6	1.21
Jim Kaat	100	20.12	John Candelaria	1	0.20
Dale Murphy	96	19.32	Mike Boddicker	0	0.00
Tommy John	93	18.71	Charlie Leibrandt	0	0.00
Dave Parker	80	16.10	Frank Tanana	0	0.00
Minnie Minoso*	73	14.69	Mike Witt	0	0.00

Bold type: Player was elected to Hall of Fame
*: Player is in 15th and final year of eligibility on the BBWAA ballot

AP/Wide World Photos

If there was ever a sure thing, Nolan Ryan and George Brett being inducted into the Hall of Fame their first time on the ballot was it. But not everybody thought so. Remember: Voting is done by media types who may carry opinions and grudges well beyond the five-year waiting period. Six voters left Ryan off the ballot, but he still received enough support to make him second highest in voting percentage. The highest: Tom Seaver, the matinee-idol pitcher of the Mets, Reds and White Sox from 1967 to 1986. Here are the highest percentages in balloting for baseball's Hall of Fame:

Player	Year	Pct.
Tom Seaver	1992	98.84
Nolan Ryan	1999	98.79
Ty Cobb	1936	98.23
George Brett	1999	98.19
Hank Aaron	1982	97.83
Mike Schmidt	1995	96.52
Johnny Bench	1989	96.42
Steve Carlton	1994	95.82
Honus Wagner	1936	95.13
Babe Ruth	1936	95.13
Willie Mays	1979	94.67
Carl Yastrzemski	1989	94.63

RYAN'S RECORDS

A SAMPLING OF THE BASEBALL RECORDS HELD BY NOLAN RYAN...

- Most strikeouts, major leagues: 5,714.
- Most strikeouts, season, major leagues: 383, California, 1973.
- Most years, 100 or more strikeouts: 24, New York Mets, 1968, '70, '71; California, 1972-79; Houston, 1980-88; Texas, 1989-92.
- Most years, 200 or more strikeouts, major leagues: 15, California, 1972-79, except 1975; Houston, 1980, '82, '85, '87, '88; Texas, 1989-91.
- Most years, 300 or more strikeouts, major leagues: 6, California, 1972, '73, '74, '76, '77; Texas, 1989.
- Most strikeouts, losing pitcher, extra-inning game, major leagues: 19, California, August 20, 1974, 11 innings, lost 1-0.
- Most times, 15 or more strikeouts, game, major leagues: 26, New York Mets, 1970 (1), 1971 (1); California, 1972 (4), 1973 (2), 1974 (6), 1976 (3), 1977 (2), 1978 (1), 1979 (1); Houston, 1987 (1); Texas, 1989 (1), 1990 (2), 1991 (1).
- Most times, 10 or more strikeouts, game, major leagues: 215, 67 in National League, New York and Houston, 13 years, 1966, '68-71, '80-88; 148 in American League, California and Texas, 12 years, 1972-79, '89-92.
- Most times, 10 or more strikeouts, game, season: 23, California, 1973.
- Three strikeouts, inning, on nine pitches*: New York Mets, April 19, 1968, third inning; California, July 9, 1972, second inning.
- Most consecutive strikeouts, game, American League: 8*, California, July 9, 1972; California, July 15, 1973.
- Oldest pitcher, 10 or more strikeouts, game: 45 years, 6 months, 6 days, August 6, 1992 vs. Oakland.
- Most no-hitters pitched, major leagues: 7, California, 1973 (2), 1974, 1975; Houston, 1981; Texas, 1990, 1991.
- Most no-hitters pitched, season: 2*, California, May 15 and July 15, 1973.
- Oldest pitcher to throw no-hitter: 44 years, 3 months, 1 day, May 1, 1991 vs. Toronto.
- Most teams, throwing no-hitter: 3, California (4); Houston, Texas (2).
- Most different decades, throwing no-hitter: 3, 1970s, '80s, '90s.
- Longest span between throwing no-hitters: 8 years, 8 months, 16 days, September 26, 1981, until June 11, 1990.
- Most one-hit games, career, major leagues: 12*.
- Most bases on balls, major leagues: 2,795
- Most clubs shut out (won or tied), season, major and American League: 8*, California, 1972.
- Most wild pitches, major leagues: 277.
- Highest strikeout average per nine innings, season: 11.48, Houston, 1987.
- Highest strikeout average per nine innings, career: 9.55, 27 seasons, 1966.
- Lowest hits allowed average per nine innings, career: 6.55, 26 seasons.
- Most consecutive starts without a relief appearance: 594, July 30, 1974-September 22, 1993.
- Most different seasons, major leagues: 27, New York Mets, 1966, 1968-71; California, 1972-79; Houston, 1980-88; Texas, 1989-93.
- Most grand slams allowed, career, major leagues: 10
- Most strikeouts, game, relief pitcher: 7, New York Mets, October 6, 1969, pitched seven innings.
- Most consecutive strikeouts, game: 4*, California, October 3, 1979.
- Most consecutive strikeouts, start of game: 4*, California, October 3, 1979.
- Highest fielding percentage, pitcher, with most chances accepted, five-game series, National League: 1.000*, Houston, 1980, four chances accepted.
- Most assists, pitcher, five-game series, National League: 3*, Houston, 1980.
- Most chances accepted, pitcher, five-game series, National League: 4*, Houston, 1980.
- Oldest pitcher to win All-Star Game: 42 years, 5 months, 13 days, July 12, 1989, at California for American League.
- Nolan Ryan holds more major league records than any other player in the game!

*—Ties record

Robin Yount (left), Nolan Ryan (center) and George Brett were all voted into the National Baseball Hall of Fame in their first year on the ballot.

Ryan received the support of 491 of 497 voters (98.79%), placing him second only to Tom Seaver (98.84%) in percentage of votes cast.

MAJOR LEAGUE CAREER STATISTICS

Year	Club	W	L	ERA	REGULAR SEASON G	GS	CG	SH	IP	H	R	ER	BB	SO
1966	New York (NL)	0	1	15.00	2	1	0	0	3.0	5	5	5	3	6
1968	New York (NL)	6	9	3.09	21	18	3	0	134.0	93	50	46	75	133
1969	New York (NL)	6	3	3.53	25	10	2	0	89.1	60	38	35	53	92
1970	New York (NL)	7	11	3.42	27	19	5	2	131.2	86	59	50	97	125
1971	New York (NL)	10	14	3.97	30	26	3	0	152.0	125	78	67	116	137
1972	California (AL)	19	16	2.28	39	39	20	9	284.0	166	80	72	157	329
1973	California (AL)	21	16	2.87	41	39	26	4	326.0	238	113	104	162	383
1974	California (AL)	22	16	2.89	42	41	26	3	332.2	221	127	107	202	367
1975	California (AL)	14	12	3.45	28	28	10	5	198.0	152	90	76	132	186
1976	California (AL)	17	18	3.36	39	39	21	7	284.1	193	117	106	183	327
1977	California (AL)	19	16	2.77	37	37	22	4	299.0	198	110	92	204	341
1978	California (AL)	10	13	3.72	31	31	14	3	234.2	183	106	97	148	260
1979	California (AL)	16	14	3.60	34	34	17	5	222.2	169	104	89	114	223
1980	Houston (NL)	11	10	3.35	35	35	4	2	233.2	205	100	87	98	200
1981	Houston (NL)	11	5	1.69	21	21	5	3	149.0	99	34	28	68	140
1982	Houston (NL)	16	12	3.16	35	35	10	3	250.1	196	100	88	109	245
1983	Houston (NL)	14	9	2.98	29	29	5	2	196.1	134	74	65	101	183
1984	Houston (NL)	12	11	3.04	30	30	5	2	183.2	143	78	62	69	197
1985	Houston (NL)	10	12	3.80	35	35	4	0	232.0	205	108	98	95	209
1986	Houston (NL)	12	8	3.34	30	30	1	0	178.0	119	72	66	82	194
1987	Houston (NL)	8	16	2.76	34	34	0	0	211.2	154	75	65	87	270
1988	Houston (NL)	12	11	3.52	33	33	4	1	220.0	186	98	86	87	228
1989	Texas (AL)	16	10	3.20	32	32	6	2	239.1	162	96	85	98	301
1990	Texas (AL)	13	9	3.44	30	30	5	2	204.0	137	86	78	74	232
1991	Texas (AL)	12	6	2.91	27	27	2	2	173.0	102	58	56	72	203
1992	Texas (AL)	5	9	3.72	27	27	2	0	157.1	138	75	65	69	157
1993	Texas (AL)	5	5	4.88	13	13	0	0	66.1	54	47	36	40	46
	AL Totals	189	160	3.17	420	417	171	46	3021.1	2113	1209	1063	1655	3355
	NL Totals	135	132	3.23	387	356	51	15	2364.2	1810	969	848	1140	2359
	Totals	324	292	3.19	807	773	222	61	5386.0	3923	2178	1911	2795	5714

DIVISIONAL SERIES

Year	Club	W	L	ERA	G	GS	CG	SH	IP	H	R	ER	BB	SO
1981	Houston (NL)	1	1	1.80	2	2	1	0	15	6	4	3	3	14

LEAGUE CHAMPIONSHIP SERIES

Year	Club	W	L	ERA	G	GS	CG	SH	IP	H	R	ER	BB	SO
1969	New York (NL)	1	0	2.57	1	0	0	0	7	3	2	2	2	7
1979	California (AL)	0	0	1.29	1	1	0	0	7	4	3	1	3	8
1980	Houston (NL)	0	0	5.40	2	2	0	0	13.1	16	8	8	3	14
1986	Houston (NL)	0	1	3.86	2	2	0	0	14	9	6	6	1	17
	Totals	1	1	3.70	6	5	0	0	41.1	32	19	17	9	46

WORLD SERIES

Year	Club	W	L	ERA	G	GS	CG	SH	IP	H	R	ER	BB	SO
1969	New York (NL)	0	0	0.00	1	0	0	0	2.1	1	0	0	2	3

Ryan stands with his namesake, the Southwest Airlines jet christened the Nolan Ryan Express in honor of the famous hurler.

AP/Wide World Photos

"He provides us with a legacy. For a franchise to have a tradition, it must have legends. Mickey Mantle, Joe DiMaggio and Babe Ruth are legends in New York. Nolan Ryan is a legend in Texas."

—George W. Bush

Louis DeLuca

Other Titles by Sports Publishing Inc.

and

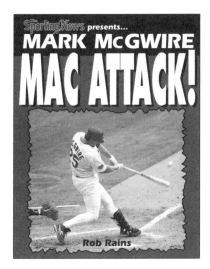

Mark McGwire: Mac Attack!

by Rob Rains

Mac Attack! describes how McGwire quickly has become a legendary figure in St. Louis, the home to baseball legends such as Stan Musial, Lou Brock, Bob Gibson, Red Schoendienst and Ozzie Smith. While growing up, McGwire thought about being a police officer, but he hit a home run in his first Little League at-bat and the rest is history.

108 pp • 5 1/2 x 7 paperback • $5.95 • Juvenile (ages 12-15)

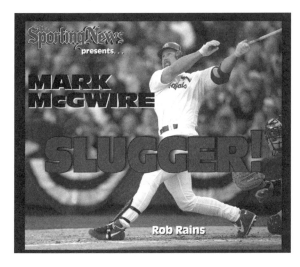

Mark McGwire: Slugger!

by Rob Rains

Slugger! describes how Mark overcame poor eyesight and various injuries to become one of baseball's most revered hitters. This inspirational book encourages children to overcome life's difficult experiences and to "never give up on following..." their dreams.

47 pp • 10 x 8 3/4 hardcover • $15.95 • Juvenile (ages 6-11)

To order call toll-free at 1-877-424-2665 or visit your local bookstore.